THE 250 POWER WORDS THAT $ELL

STEPHAN SCHIFFMAN
America's #1 Corporate Sales Trainer

THE 250 POWER WORDS THAT $ELL

The Words You Need to *GET THE SALE, BEAT YOUR QUOTA,* and *BOOST YOUR COMMISSION*

Aadamsmedia
Avon, Massachusetts

Published by
Adams Media, a division of F+W Media, Inc.
57 Littlefield Street, Avon, MA 02322. U.S.A.
www.adamsmedia.com

Contains material adapted and abridged from *The 25 Sales Strategies That Will Boost Your Sales Today!*, by Stephan Schiffman, copyright © 1999 by Stephan Schiffman, ISBN 10: 1-58062-116-3, ISBN 13: 978-1-58062-116-8; *The 25 Sales Skills They Don't Teach at Business School*, by Stephan Schiffman, copyright © 2002 by D.E.I. Management Group, ISBN 10: 1-58062-614-9, ISBN 13: 978-1-58062-614-9; *The 25 Sales Habits of Highly Successful Salespeople*, 3rd edition, by Stephan Schiffman, copyright © 1990, 2008 by Stephan Schiffman, ISBN 10: 1-59869-757-9, ISBN 13: 978-1-59869-757-5; *The 25 Most Common Sales Mistakes and How to Avoid Them*, 3rd edition, by Stephan Schiffman, copyright 1991, 2009 by Stephan Schiffman, ISBN 10: 1-59869-821-4, ISBN 13: 978-1-59869-821-3; *Cold Calling Techniques (That Really Work!)*, 20th anniversary edition, by Stephan Schiffman, copyright © 1987, 2007, by Stephan Schiffman, ISBN 10: 1-59869-148-1, ISBN 13: 978-1-59869-148-1; *Closing Techniques (That Really Work!)*, 4th edition, by Stephan Schiffman, copyright © 2009 by Stephan Schiffman, ISBN 10: 1-59869-820-6, ISBN 13: 978-1-59869-820-6; *Sales Presentation Techniques (That Really Work!)*, by Stephan Schiffman, copyright © 2007, by Stephan Schiffman, ISBN 10: 1-59869-060-4, ISBN 13: 978-1-59869-060-6; *E-mail Selling Techniques (That Really Work!)*, by Stephan Schiffman, copyright © by Stephan Schiffman, ISBN 10: 1-59337-744-4, ISBN 13: 978-1-59337-744-1; *Ask Questions, Get Sales*, 2nd edition, by Stephan Schiffman, copyright © 2005 Stephan Schiffman, ISBN 10: 1-59337-112-8, ISBN 13: 978-1-59337-112-8.

ISBN 10: 1-4405-5625-3
ISBN 13: 978-1-4405-5625-8
eISBN 10: 1-4405-5626-1
eISBN 13: 978-1-4405-5626-5

Printed in the United States of America.

10   9   8   7   6   5   4   3   2   1

This book is available at quantity discounts for bulk purchases.
For information, please call 1-800-289-0963.

Contents

Introduction 7

PART I **WHAT TO SAY WHEN YOU'RE PROSPECTING** 9

CHAPTER 1 *The Right Words for a Cold Call* 11
CHAPTER 2 *How to Leave an Effective Voicemail* 23
CHAPTER 3 *The Best Words for E-mails* 41
CHAPTER 4 *Turning Around Common Responses* 57

PART II **WHAT TO SAY WHEN YOU'RE INTERVIEWING** . .71

CHAPTER 5 *Getting the Interview Going* 73
CHAPTER 6 *Six Basic Questions* 81
CHAPTER 7 *The Power of Framing* 93
CHAPTER 8 *Finding Out about the Past and Future* 105
CHAPTER 9 *The Art of Small Talk (That Isn't Small)* 117

PART III **WHAT TO SAY WHEN YOU'RE PRESENTING** . . 143

CHAPTER 10 *Active Listening* 145

CHAPTER 11 *What to Tell Prospects* **151**

CHAPTER 12 *The Reason You're There* **157**

PART IV **WHAT TO SAY WHEN YOU'RE CLOSING** **169**

CHAPTER 13 *Overcoming Common Objections* **171**

CHAPTER 14 *Ask for the Deal* **183**

CHAPTER 15 *Follow Up with a Flourish* **189**

Conclusion **195**

APPENDIX *Sample Sales Dialogues* **201**

Index **219**

Introduction

"What is your company doing now?"
"Premier manufacturer of these products"
"Benefits"
"Features"
"Increased profits"
"We should get together and talk."

What do these words and phrases mean to you? Do you use them during cold calling, sales presentations, or when you're closing a deal? What kind of words do you use to elicit a strong response—positive or negative—from your prospects?

Words are the basic tools of your trade. They're what make a sale happen. And the better you are at using them, the more successful your professional life will be. In fact, this is true for just about any trade or profession. For example:

The next time you have occasion to call a professional into your home to fix something—a plumber, say—watch him while he works. What will strike you is that he's extremely precise in his movements. There's no wasted motion or effort. And a big part of that is that he has his toolbox open beside him and obviously knows where each tool is and what he'll need it for. He barely looks as he reaches time and again into the box to pull out now a wrench, now a pair of pliers. And in what often seems like very little time, he's packing up his tools, being careful to put each item away in its designated spot.

Like the plumber, you need to have all your tools—that is to say, your words—neatly arranged where you can find them and use them. Also like the plumber, you need to know which words are appropriate to each given situation. This book will teach you how to do that and how to choose the best words for any part of the sales cycle.

These are the four parts of any sale: Prospecting, Interviewing, Presenting, and Closing. Your success as a salesperson depends in large part on understanding what each one of these components does and how it works with the other three. You've got to keep your word tools organized and understand how to use them effectively.

If a plumber stopped keeping his tools organized and went to jobs with his tools tossed willy-nilly in his toolbox, he'd be constantly groping for the right tool. Each job would take longer and be a less efficient use of his time and skills. He might, of course, get the job done, but people would be less inclined to hire him; after all, who wants a plumber who takes the entire day to fix a simple leak?

In the same way, when you're selling you should always use the right words for the right job. You should know where they are and what they do. And in the same way as a successful plumber can stop a leak, unplug a sink, or install a bathtub with little mess and fuss, you'll be able to improve your sales and increase your commission with the aid of the right words.

Good luck!

PART I

WHAT TO SAY WHEN YOU'RE PROSPECTING

Prospecting is essential to the sales cycle. It's something salespeople should do—must do—every day. Elsewhere I've talked about the importance of keeping up your numbers, your cold-call-to-appointments ratio. As we'll see, choosing the right words is an invaluable tool in that process.

CHAPTER 1

The Right Words for a Cold Call

Cold calling is one of the most basic parts of the sales process. The cold call plays an essential role in successful prospecting. It's the best and most economical way for you to develop sales leads into prospects on an ongoing basis. And it's a place where using the right words and phrases can make a huge difference in how the call goes.

- In the introduction: **Hello, Mr. Smith. My name's Bob Johnson.**
- In the reason for your call: **I'd like to talk to you about improving your sales performance by at least 25 percent.**
- In asking for an appointment: **We've got a lot to talk about, Mr. Smith. How about meeting this Friday at 2:00 P.M.?**

This may seem simple, but straying too much from these key words and phrases can cause your cold call to go badly off track. Above all, you have to keep this in mind: When you're following up with leads, your first and most important step is to get the appointment. So the main task of a cold call is to get an appointment. It's as simple as that.

Cold Call Mechanics

There are five basic elements to the initial cold call:

1. Get the person's attention
2. Identify yourself and your company
3. Give the reason for your call
4. Make a qualifying/questioning statement
5. Set the appointment

I'm going to cover these in order, explaining key words and phrases that are appropriate to each element.

Here then are the five elements.

1. Get the Person's Attention

Let's assume I'm calling you. Depending upon what I say, you're going to respond. No matter what I say, you're going to respond somehow. And the better I get at my opening, the more likely I am to get a good response from you!

People Respond in Kind

When you try to get the person's attention, remember that people respond in kind. Most salespeople think they have to say something unique or provocative to grab a prospect's attention. The easiest, simplest way of opening up and getting the prospect's attention is by saying his or her name. Call up and say, **"Good morning, Mr. Jones."**

Words and Phrases to Introduce Yourself

Good morning
Good afternoon
How are you?
It's good to speak with you

Always remember to follow any of these openings with the lead's name. That's the most important thing you can do.

The opening of your call is going to lead to a response. You can anticipate that response. You are then going to produce an appropriate turnaround, which should get the appointment. The key to the call is actually not the opening. The reality is no matter what you say in the opening, people are going to respond to you, and you can prepare for those responses.

2. Identify Yourself and Your Company

If I called you up and simply said, "Good morning, Mr. Jones, this is Steve Schiffman from D.E.I. Franchise Systems, Inc.," you probably would not know who I was—or what D.E.I. Franchise Systems, Inc. was—and you probably wouldn't give me the kind of response I wanted. Therefore, I have to go further. I have to build a brief introduction, or *commercial*, into the call. For example, I could say, **"Good morning, Mr. Jones, this is Steve Schiffman from D.E.I. here in New York City. We're a major sales training company that's worked with over 500,000 salespeople."**

Words and Phrases to Identify You and Your Company

This is John Johnson from the XYZ Company. We specialize in information systems maintenance and repair.

This is Alice Allison from ABC Company, Inc. We're a nationwide dealership in used electronics.

We make

We create

We service

We provide

We assemble

We manufacture

We innovate
We communicate

In each of these cases, the second sentence distills down the essence of what your company does. Notice that the second word is always a verb, one that captures the essence of what your company does. There's no need for a long explanation, which is going to derail the call and give your lead more information than she or he wants at present. Avoid something like:

Good morning, Mr. Jones. My name is David Davidson from ClickClack Company. We do a lot of our business in the Midwest, servicing farm implements. We have offices in Cincinnati, Kansas City, Omaha, and Sioux City, Iowa. We have over 800 employees, and we offer full-service contracts every year for more than 10,000 machines in the following states . . .

"Click." The lead has already hung up. You gave too much information at the wrong time. For right now, keep it simple and one sentence long.

3. Give the Reason for Your Call

Now, the third step, the reason for the call, becomes important. Of course, if you make enough cold calls, you'll get some kind of response. What we're interested in here is improving the response you get.

When calling for an appointment, I suggest you say the following: **"The reason I'm calling you today specifically is to set an appointment."**

Now, if that were all I said, if that were my entire program, what do you think would happen? I would get appointments.

If I simply say, "The reason I'm calling today is to set an appointment," someone will see me. In fact, my experience is that something like one person out of twelve will see you simply because that person is not sure what you're calling about and will agree to meet with you *because you asked*. Now do you see why it begins to make sense just to ask for an appointment in a straightforward way?

I can enhance that third element of the script. Instead of simply saying, "The reason I'm calling is to set an appointment," I can turn it into something more compelling by saying, for instance, **"The reason I'm calling you today specifically is to set an appointment so I can stop by and tell you about our new sales training programs and how they can increase the productivity of your sales force."**

Notice that what I've just said paints a picture for Mr. Jones. I've really given him a reason for my call. I've talked about increasing productivity. I've actually given him some reasons we should get together.

Words and Phrases to Say Why You Called

The reason I'm calling you today is to set up an appointment

Our program can benefit your company

My company's systems can increase your workforce productivity

We'll work with you to develop new customer service solutions

improve
expand
further develop

4. Make a Questioning or Qualifying Statement

Now, I'm going to add a questioning statement that's going to allow the prospect an opportunity to respond to me in kind—favorably. The question that I'm going to ask has to be based on my reason for calling Mr. Jones.

My qualifying or questioning statement has to follow easily and logically from that statement. It has to be a reasonable and nonmanipulative extension of what's come before.

I can start out with, **"Mr. Jones, I'm sure that you, like a lot of the other companies that I work with . . ."** and here I insert some real names. I might mention a computer company, an HMO, or a life insurance company. It could sound like this: **"I'm sure that you, like ABC Company, are interested in having a more effective sales staff."** We now have a name inserted as a reference. Mr. Jones is much more likely to say, "Yes, I'm interested."

Words and Phrases for a Questioning Statement

Like the XYZ Corporation, I'm sure you'd be interested in improving your customer service response times.

Since the BigSales Corporation has increased its market penetration by more than 15 percent, I'm sure you'd like to match them in that.

Would you be interested, like the ABC Company, in see-ing a growth in your door-to-door delivery times of around 20 percent?
   expanded its area
   increased sales
   more effective staff
   developed outreach

5. Set the Appointment

Now I'm ready to set the appointment. Here's how:

"That's great, Mr. Jones, then we should get together. How about Tuesday at 3:00 P.M.?"

That's it. Look at it again! You are simply going to say some-thing like the following: "That's great, Mr. Jones, then we should get together. How's Tuesday at 3:00 P.M.?" Be specific. The request *must* be this direct, this brief, and this specific. Don't change it!

The discussion should focus on *when* we're going to get together, not *whether* we're going to get together. Now I have a better chance of getting the appointment.

The biggest mistake most salespeople make is that they fail to ask directly and specifically for the appointment. When I say, "Let's get together Tuesday at 3:00 P.M.," I'm being spe-cific, and I'm going to get a response in kind—that is, a spe-cific answer about the appointment on Tuesday at 3:00 P.M.—because as I told you earlier, people respond in kind.

Words and Phrases to Get the Appointment

We should talk further. How's Monday at 4:00 P.M.?

We certainly have a lot to discuss. Are you free Tuesday at noon?

I'd like this to be the basis for further discussion. Shall we say Friday at 9:00 A.M.?

Let's talk more about this Wednesday at 2:00 P.M.

Now let's put all this together. Before we do so, though, I want to emphasize the value of using a script.

"But I Don't Want to Use a Script!"

Have you recently seen a movie or a television show that you really enjoyed? Sure you have. Did the actors in that drama or that comedy sound like they were reading from a script? No. It doesn't sound like a script because the actor has internalized what has to be said. That's what you must do. You should use a script, but you don't have to just read mechanically from the paper in front of you. Instead, you have to internalize what you're going to say so it sounds natural.

For example, I've been teaching the *Cold Calling Techniques* program for years. I've learned it, I've memorized it, and I've internalized it. I can, therefore, take that program and change it and adjust it as the circumstances require. It always sounds natural.

The objective here is not to "handcuff" you with a script. The objective is to help you develop a script that will help you say what you need to say, while freeing you to pay attention to the prospect's response, which is what's really important.

What is the response? What is the person saying? Are we creating an atmosphere that will make it easy to prompt positive responses? Or are people responding negatively because we've asked the wrong questions, or asked the right questions in the wrong way? Using a script makes it easier for you to listen for crucial information, since you know exactly what you're going to say.

Sample Cold Call

Here's how a successful cold call might go:

You: **Good morning, Mr. Johnson.**

Mr. Johnson: Good morning.

You: This is Jane Smith, of Smith and Parkinson Accounting. **We're an accounting partnership of CPAs who specialize in companies such as yours** that develop and market intellectual properties.

Mr. Johnson: What can I do for you, Ms. Smith?

You: I'm calling you today to set up an appointment to discuss **how my company can create significant savings** of up to 15 percent for you in the areas of accounting and taxes. I'm sure you're aware that the recent revisions to the tax code have made matters somewhat more complicated for those companies that deal in intellectual properties, and **good accounting can be a significant competitive advantage**. You may not be aware that the Big Game Company has increased its profitability by 10 percent, and **a significant portion of that was due to cost savings developed by their accounting firm**.

Mr. Johnson: That's interesting. I hadn't realized that.

You: I'd like to **discuss this with you in more detail. How's Tuesday afternoon** at 2:00 P.M.?

Mr. Johnson: That should be okay. I'll switch you to my admin to set up the appointment.

You: Thank you, Mr. Johnson. **I look forward to seeing you** on Tuesday.

Keep it short and sweet. Remember: The main task of the cold call is to get the appointment. Once you've done that, politely end the call and start preparing for the next step in the sales cycle.

CHAPTER 2

How to Leave an Effective Voicemail

I'm always a little bit mystified when I run into salespeople who tell me they "don't believe" in voicemail messages when it comes to making prospecting calls. Nowadays, that's a little bit like saying you don't believe in the planet Earth.

All the same, there are a good many salespeople we train who swear that it's a waste of time to leave messages for prospects. I have a sneaking suspicion that these salespeople simply don't like making prospecting calls in the first place. Reaching someone's voicemail is common now. But if you're going to persuade people not to hit the "delete" button on their phone before they even finish listening to your message, you're going to have to figure out what kind of message to leave. And the key to that is knowing which words to use.

Some salespeople think they can overcome the voicemail problem by sheer volume. They overcall cold contacts, and leave two, three, five, or even more voicemail messages per week. They use every word they can think of—and some they haven't used in a long time. This method of using voicemail is not only a huge waste of time but is also a poor way to initiate a business relationship. Think back on the last time you received three or more consecutive voicemail messages in a single week from someone you didn't know. Were you more or less likely to return the person's calls at the end of the week?

In this chapter, I'm going to show you how to leave succinct, powerful, and informative voicemail messages by paying close attention to your language. If you do this, you'll leave no more than one voicemail message per business week when trying to establish connection with a new contact. And that's all you should leave.

(*Note*: The situation is different, of course, once you've established some kind of "next step" with the person in question. At that point, you're dealing with an active prospect. It's quite common for people with busy schedules to exchange three or four messages before connecting in person or by phone, and some business relationships will actually unfold almost exclusively by means of voicemail or some other messaging option. The point is there's a different standard once you've gotten the contact to agree to meet with you in person.)

The Two Ways to Leave a Voicemail

In the age of voicemail, you must know how to leave a message that can increase your chances of having the person get back to you. I'm going to give you two specific, very effective ways to leave a message. The first way will give you between 65 to 75 percent return calls. The second way is almost 99 percent effective!

Calling with a Company Name

Here's the first way—the way that most representatives we train leave messages.

Let's say I'm calling someone, and the admin or receptionist tells me I'm going to have to leave a message. If you recall what I said in the previous chapter, the central reason for my calling is the success I had with the XYZ Company. Therefore, my referring comment or my reference point should be the XYZ Company. So my message will sound like this:

"This is Steve Schiffman from D.E.I. Franchise Systems, Inc.; my telephone number is 212-555-1234. Would you

please tell him it's in reference to the XYZ Company." If I reach an automated voicemail system instead of an actual person, the method's essentially the same, but a bit more concise: **"This is Steve Schiffman from D.E.I. Franchise Systems, Inc.; my phone number is 212-555-1212. It's regarding XYZ Company."**

So the essential components are:

1. My name
2. My company affiliation
3. My phone number
4. A third-party reference

Notice that I don't give a lot of detail or other information, which will probably lead him to hang up or push "delete" before he's listened to the whole message. My message takes between ten to fifteen seconds, maximum.

Words and Phrases to Leave a Message or Voicemail

My name is [x]
I'm from XYZ Company
My phone number is [x]
concerning
with regard to

When the prospect calls me back, I'm going to say: **"Oh, I'm glad you called me. The reason I called you is that we recently did a project with the XYZ Company."**

And then I immediately go into my call about being successful with the XYZ Company. I have to carry that through. If I don't then the calls will not be consistent.

You can't lie or mislead. You must leave your company's name as well as the referring company's. You must be precise, and you must make sure that the secretary or the assistant gets the name of your company. Be careful *not* to give the impression that you represent the XYZ Company. If you do that, you will have trouble later on. Maybe not on your first call or your second call, but eventually someone's going to say you misled them, and they'll be right.

You don't have to use a huge company for this strategy to work. It doesn't matter whether or not the person even knows the company as long as you get him or her on the phone. You can use a company that you're familiar with or a company that your contact should be familiar with, but isn't. In the somewhat unlikely event that the person says to you, "Well, I don't know anything about the XYZ Company," you can start by saying, **"Oh, well they're the biggest widget company in the area. They do A, B, and C. Anyway, the reason I was calling you . . ."** and then you can go right into your opening.

It doesn't even matter if the person tells you that he doesn't really care about that company because now you're on the phone together. You can say, **"Oh, that's all right. I'm just curious, though. What do you do?"** And you're going to use their answer to create the ledge for yourself. So it doesn't really matter how people respond to the message you leave—whether that response is positive or negative—as long as they call you back.

Words and Phrases for the Follow-Up Phone Conversation

What we were able to do for XYZ Company
We were able to help the company
grow the company
expand
develop
What do you do?

We get 65 to 75 percent of our calls returned using this method.

Calling with an Individual's Name

The second method of leaving a message came to me in an interesting way.

Every once in a while it's necessary to terminate someone; sometimes people just leave. That's just the way things go. Some years ago, when I was running my company I had a representative working for me who didn't work out—I'm going to call him Bob Jones. After Bob left the company, I started thinking that, as president, I really should call everybody Bob had ever talked to in order to see whether I could start the conversation again.

The first company I called was a huge telecommunications company that Bob had met with; the headquarters were not far from our office in Manhattan. I asked to speak to the president of the company; the secretary got on the phone and said to me, "I'm sorry, he's busy. What's it in reference to?" Now remember, I usually say that my name is Steve Schiffman, my company is

D.E.I. Franchise Systems, Inc., my telephone number is . . . and I go on to mention the referring company. But in this case I had Bob Jones on my mind. I had been thinking about him for some time, because it was a little bit frustrating to me that he hadn't worked out. So I simply said that Bob Jones was my reason for calling. The secretary took the message.

About twenty minutes later, the president of the company called me back and said, "You had called me in reference to Bob Jones."

I said, **"Oh, yes. Bob Jones worked for our company a number of weeks ago. He's no longer with us, and the reason I was calling you today is we've been very successful working with the ABC Bank. I'd like to stop by next Tuesday at 3:00 P.M. and tell you about our success with them."**

He gave me the appointment, and we eventually started a business relationship.

I started thinking about that, about how many other people Bob had met with. And so I called everybody and nearly every single person—almost 100 percent—called me back. I used the same message every time, referring to Bob Jones. Now, I don't know whether or not they really remembered Bob Jones, nor do I care. I never asked that question. And when I showed up for an appointment, sometimes he would come up in conversation and sometimes he wouldn't. But they virtually all called me back. So I asked myself: How else can I use this approach?

Maria, a sales rep who's been with us for about a year, was very frustrated because she had gone on a major sales call and the person she had met with decided to stop returning her calls. I called her contact's office and said, **"My name is Steve Schiffman. My company is D.E.I. Franchise Systems,**

Inc. My number in New York is 212-555-1234. Would you please tell him it's in reference to Maria." (And I gave Maria's last name.)

Thirty-five minutes later he called me back.

Customer: You called me in reference to Maria?

Steve: Yes, you had met with Maria a number of months ago.

Customer: Oh, yes.

Steve: Anyway, **I wanted to find out what happened**.

And he told me the story. I found out that the sale was over, but the fact is I got him on the phone in under an hour. (Maria had told me that was impossible.)

You can use this technique in a lot of different situations. Have your manager call contacts at those organizations where the sale did not happen.

Words and Phrases Using an Individual's Name

I understand that you worked with Jan Smith, one of our representatives

Can you tell me why you didn't buy from Ms. Smith?

Our salesperson Michael Jones called you

What happened with Ms. Smith?

How'd Mr. Jones work with you?

I'd like to talk to you about Mr. Robinson, our lead salesperson

In other words, make the assumption that your organization did something wrong. That's a lot better than saying the prospect did something wrong! Virtually every time, this is what your sales manager will hear:

Prospect: Oh, no, Jan was great! It's just that we had these three problems, A, B, and C.

You (or your boss, if you're the one who didn't get the sale) can then say:

Oh, then we *should* get together, because **we've been working with other companies who've had the same situation**. How about next Tuesday at 3:00 P.M.?

Working as a Team

Another way to use this technique is for two reps to trade off names. I've had a number of salespeople whom I've trained do this. Ross will make the initial call. Sometimes, for whatever reason, he does not get through and the person he's trying to reach doesn't call him back. Now Melody uses Ross's name to call. Her message will be, **"This is Melody from D.E.I. calling in reference to Ross."**

This is all perfectly legitimate. Ross *had* called, and the contact never called him back. We don't know why not. When she gets the prospect on the phone, Melody simply says, **"Ross from our office had called you. I'd like to stop by."**

Typically, they'll call back and she'll get the appointment. So does Ross, but he does it in reverse, using Melody's name. You can use this method with your colleagues, or your manager can work with you.

Words and Phrases for Team Calling
John from our office called **I'd like to talk to you**

What's a good time for us to meet?
We should get together
Can we meet to discuss what happened?
My telephone number is
My contact information is

There are many different ways to use this technique. For example, you can call all of the companies that other representatives in your company have called and have not been successful with.

Let's say two years ago Jimmy Jones picked up the phone and called the Umbrella Company of America. He never got through. You want to call again. Simply use Jimmy Jones's name in your message:

"Hi, would you please tell him I called? My name is Chris Smith from the XYZ Company. My phone number is 555-1212. Would you please tell him it's in reference to Jimmy Jones."

When the prospect calls back, you're going to say:

"Hi, you had spoken to Jimmy Jones from my company a number of years ago. The reason I'm calling is that we've been very successful with the ABC Widget Company. I'd like to stop by . . ."

The strategy I've outlined makes it easy to get return calls almost 100 percent of the time, and it virtually eliminates problems with gatekeepers.

Every once in a while, an admin asks me what my call is in reference to. I simply reply that it's a long story. If pressed, I ask the admin whether he or she wants to hear the whole story. Most of the time they say "no."

I always leave a message, either with a human being or a voicemail system.

Dealing with Telephone Tag

We call somebody over and over again; they call us, but we can't seem to connect. How do you handle that?

Salespeople face this obstacle every day. We probably won't reach up to one-third of all the people we actually call simply because they didn't answer the phone. They're busy, or they're away, or they are in a meeting. You trade calls back and forth. This can be very frustrating.

My whole approach to appointment making is based on the assumption that the prospect and I ought to get together. After all, why would I doubt that? So I'm going to use that assumption in dealing with telephone tag problems.

I've called the prospect, I've expressed interest in our getting together, and in making an appointment to meet.

The prospect has also expressed some interest. Whether or not this person directly said, "I'm interested," the contact has *not* said to me, "No, I'll never see you," or "No, never call me again." Most people respond—in kind—by either saying, "No, this is not the best time," or by making an appointment.

What's really happening in telephone tag? The problem is that you have not really connected with a prospect. If you do connect, then you're going to set up a meeting. But do you really have to connect, or can you simply use the resources at hand to set the appointment?

Consider this sample call:

Steve: **Mr. Jones, the reason I'm calling you is to set an appointment.**

Mr. Jones: Please call me back.

I call Mr. Jones back in three weeks or in six months, depending on what his time frame is. What do I say? Listen:

Steve: **Mr. Jones, the reason I'm calling you specifically is that when we spoke in May you suggested I give you a call today to set up an appointment. Would next Tuesday be okay?**

That's a highly effective follow-up call.

But let's say that, for whatever reason, I don't get to talk to Mr. Jones when I call back, so I leave the following message on Mr. Jones's voicemail.

"Hi, Mr. Jones. Steve Schiffman here, from D.E.I. The reason I called is that when we spoke in May you suggested I call today to set up an appointment. I looked in my schedule and I see that I'm going to be in Philadelphia next Thursday, and I wanted to know if next Thursday at 2:30 is okay. My number is 212-555-1234."

That's the entire call. The approach uses the assumption that this person and I are in fact going to get together. (Again: Why *not* assume that?) This approach can be used with voicemail or with a secretary. You and the prospect have simply missed each other.

So refer to your first call in your follow-up call. (Never skip the first call or make untrue statements about whether you've called in the past.) Give a reason to set the appointment that day—because you're going to be in Philadelphia. (Never say, "I'm going to be in the neighborhood." That makes it sound like you're driving around Philadelphia with time on your hands. I don't think that's the message you want to send!)

Be specific. Say, "I'm going to be in Philadelphia next Thursday. I'm meeting with the XYZ Company. I could see you at 2:00 P.M., is that okay?" That kind of call will get a better response. Anything specific you can add usually gets a better response: "I'm going to be in Los Angeles a week from Friday to see the XYZ Company. Could we get together right after that?"

That's the kind of call you want to make. It sounds professional, organized, and respectful.

Words and Phrases to Stop Telephone Tag

Can we set up a time to meet?
I'd like to set up an appointment through your assistant
How's Tuesday at 10 A.M.?
When we last spoke
I'll be in Boston this Friday
meeting
get together
appointment time

Remember, the more specific you are, the greater the chance that the meeting you're trying to set up will actually come off. And in the end, that's the result you want.

Cold Calling Messages

Now let me show you how to use this method *without* any previous contact. Let's say that I'm calling a company that I want to do business with. For whatever reason, the contact is not taking my call. Perhaps he's not interested. If that's so, I want to know that.

I just simply call up and say, "Hi, this is Steve Schiffman." Whether I've reached voicemail or an assistant doesn't matter. The message should sound something like this:

"This is Steve Schiffman. I just looked at my schedule. I realize I'm going to be in Philadelphia next week to see the XYZ Company. I'll be about 20 minutes from your place. I'd like to get together. Would next Thursday about 2:30 work out?"

Now the person has to react—you've put the ball in his court. He's got to deal with you either by making an appointment or not making an appointment. Obviously, you're not going to go over unless the person agrees to see you. And I'm not suggesting that you go on an appointment simply for the sake of putting mileage on your car. I am saying, though, that you can often set up a good appointment through voicemail or by leaving a message with a secretary using the strategies I've outlined.

Suppose you've just set up your first appointment in Philadelphia. You can think to yourself, "Okay, now that I've set up this appointment in the Philadelphia area, why don't I begin to set up more meetings for Philadelphia?" Now you can call all the prospects you have in Philadelphia, all the people that you're talking with in Philadelphia, and all the people you've ever called or anybody in your office has ever called in Philadelphia. Use the methods I've given you to make those calls and set up more appointments.

Now your calls sound like this:

"I'm going to be in Philadelphia, let's get together."

Suddenly you have a good reason to call a prospect back. You have a reason to make follow-up calls. You can now set up a major sales effort in Philadelphia!

Telephone tag problems are easy to solve if you understand the big concept: The person has asked you to call back and, therefore, you're calling back. You don't necessarily have to speak to the individual directly—you can simply set the appointment.

Sometimes it's easier to understand this process by looking at the entire sequence of events. Consider this series of calls, for instance.

The first time I call, I don't get through, so I leave a message:

"Hi, this is Steve Schiffman. I'm calling in reference to Jim Jones."

"I'm calling in reference to XYZ Company."

"I'm calling because the last time we spoke . . ."

Either way, the person calls me back. If I miss the call because I'm busy going on appointments, I call the person back again. Now they call me back. So: I've called them, they've called me; I've called them, they've called me. On the third call I leave my message:

"Hi, Mr. Jones, this is Steve Schiffman. The reason I was calling you is to set an appointment. Would next Tuesday at 2:00 P.M. be okay?"

Again, I can do this either with voicemail or I can do it with an assistant. I can use the same message if I happen to get through to the person I want to talk to. The fact is I've shortened my message. I don't need to leave a longer message because I've already called. My assumption is that the prospect is going to see me, so I ask: **"Can we get together next Tuesday at 2:00 P.M.?"**

This is the single best way to defeat telephone tag. It's breathtaking in its simplicity. And it works!

Voicemail should never be an obstacle for you when making a sales call. In fact, it's a challenge because it forces you to compress your message down to the smallest possible space. And what is that message? You want to set up an appointment. This is the most important thing you're doing during your call. It's how great salespeople turn prospects into clients.

Sample Voicemail and Follow-Up

Voicemail

Hi, Roger, this is **Steve Jones of ABC Company**. I'm calling **concerning the RXJ Corporation** with whom you do a lot of business. Sorry you're not in, but **please contact me at 555-123-5577**. I'd like to **set up an appointment** with you for further discussion.

Follow-up

Steve: Hello? Steve Jones here.

Roger: Hi, Steve, this is Roger Marks from Consolidated Industries. You called the other day about RXJ Corporation.

Steve: Yes, I did. **Thanks very much for getting back to me.** I know your company has done a lot of business with RXJ over the years.

Roger: Right.

Steve: My company, ABC, has **worked very closely with RXJ** during the past two years on their internal accounting systems, and we've been able to **make substantial efficiencies for**

them in a number of areas across the company. **I'd like to have a meeting with you to discuss how we can offer the same service to Consolidated Industries.** Would this **Tuesday at 10:00 A.M.** work for you?

Roger: Okay. I'm going to switch you to my assistant, and he'll set it up.

Steve: Thanks very much. **I look forward to seeing you then**.

CHAPTER 3

The Best Words for E-mails

Although I have to confess that I generally don't like e-mail selling, more and more people seem to be using it. Many of them rely exclusively on it—a big mistake in my opinion. But I have come to think that there's a place for e-mail in the sales cycle. I've even written a book about it, *E-mail Selling Techniques (That Really Work!)*. In this chapter I want to present you with some basic principles, words, and phrases for constructing effective e-mails. Words are essential here, and they're too often forgotten because too many e-mails are hastily composed and even more hastily sent.

So I suggest you take a deep breath, sit back, and take your finger off the "Send" key. Let's look at how to write an effective e-mail message.

Obviously there is no single perfect e-mail message that is applicable to all situations where we have the opportunity to move the sale cycle forward. There is, however, a set of standards we can apply to most of the e-mail messages that go out to prospects when we hit "send." I want to share those with you now.

There are basically three questions that we have to answer. They are:

1. How *long* should the message be?
2. How *detailed* should the message be?
3. How *casual* should the message be?

I want to take you through these in order and share some thoughts on the types of answers that you should be giving as you create your messages.

Let us look at the first question: *How long should the message be?*

The best answer is: pretty darn short.

As a general rule, the *only* people I will read long e-mail messages from are people who are either my customers or people I am related to by blood. When it comes to anyone else, I either skip the message entirely or read the beginning and the ending and decide from there what I should do.

Be honest. This is probably very similar to your own standard. My guess is that, in your world, the only people whose long messages do get read are those from your own customers, your boss, or your relatives. (And let's be honest again: We may not read every single solitary word of some of those messages from the people we are related to, either.)

So we're creating messages that we want people to read. It is incumbent on us to keep our messages short if we want to get anything accomplished by means of an e-mail message that moves the sales process forward. How short? Again, think in terms of a single computer screen.

Everybody who uses e-mail uses it in one of two ways these days: either by means of looking at a computer screen or by looking at a display that is considerably smaller, like a smartphone. That means that we who write messages actually have a very small amount of space in which to make our point. For my money, it is best to keep messages so short as to be impossible *not* to read if you glance at them—two to three sentences tops for the main portion of the message. Note that I am talking about the message that shows up in the body of the e-mail and not the subject line or the signature, which are separate animals.

Here's the second question: *How detailed should the message be?* The answer here is that the message should go into relevant detail and feature a few of those details. For instance, the message can emphasize that we have worked with a company in this prospective customer's industry. In other words, we want to be just as detailed as it takes to provoke curiosity and get a response—but be no more detailed than that.

Let's look at the third question: *How casual should we be?* This is a very difficult question because the e-mail message has become, for so many of us, a replacement for verbal interaction. That means that during the course of our working day, we are sending around casual e-mail messages to friends and coworkers. We may be tempted to adopt the same level of discourse that we would use if we were hanging around the water cooler. But in fact, if we are reaching out to a brand-new person or someone we have only recently spoken to on the phone, we actually have to assume a somewhat higher standard.

The Subject Line

Let's start with one of the most important parts of the message: the subject line.

In fact, *the most important part of the e-mail message*, and the part that I would urge you to pay attention to and strategize more closely than any other part, is the subject line.

Here are some examples of subject lines sent by real, live salespeople that are well intentioned enough but still fail miserably at the task of getting the person to open the message and consider its contents.

Subject: Article

Is this a request that I send the person an article? Is this a request that the person be allowed to interview me for an article? Is this a request for an article that I have written?

Subject: Your company's success

There's nothing misleading about this. The salesperson really does want to talk to me about my company's success in the body of the e-mail. But what possible entry point to this subject does the single sentence here give me? My company's success depends on any one of a thousand different factors and all I get from a subject heading like this is that the person who's e-mailing me isn't willing to specify which one of those thousands of factors this message relates to.

This is another subject heading that is so vague that it undercuts any actual content of the body of the message that might be of interest to me. In fact, the person was trying to meet with me to discuss ways for me to expand my network of sales training franchises by means of display advertising. I'm not saying he necessarily had to put the words **display advertising** in the heading, but might it have made sense to connect the heading somehow to the goal I already knew about—namely, expanding my franchise network?

Subject: Tomorrow

This is an example of a subject line that is self-contained and has no meaningful connection whatsoever to the message it precedes. If I recognized who the message was coming from, this could be a great heading because I would be interested in finding out what the person had to say about tomorrow. But in this case, I had no idea who this person was, and so I was left a message from a stranger about something unspecified that would happen tomorrow. The person who was planning to call "tomorrow" wanted to discuss my investments. I missed the call.

Strong Subject Lines

So much for well-meaning headlines that fail to engage the recipient. What do the best subject lines look like?

Here is one of my favorites:

Subject: June 23 meeting

The beauty of this heading is that it immediately answers the first question that everybody has when they are considering opening up an e-mail message, namely, "Is this something I really have to look at?"

In this case, the message makes it clear that it is something that requires attention, because there is a meeting in the short term. In fact, when I send this message, what I am doing is asking the person whether or not he or she is willing to meet with me on a certain date and time. I particularly like placing an emphasis on times and dates and months in headings, because it causes the recipient to wonder whether or not the message affects his or her immediate schedule. And by immediate schedule, I mean something that takes place during the next two weeks.

Commitments that take place within this particular time frame tend to mean much more than commitments that are made for three months or six months or nine months or twelve months away. The closer we get to that two-week time frame, the more meaningful that commitment is and the more important the communication about it becomes. So it stands to reason that a heading that focuses on a specific date within the next two weeks will probably have more interest than something that does not.

Here is another heading that works:

Subject: Joe Clark

This subject line is a good one to use when Joe Clark is someone known to both the sender and the recipient of the message. If Joe Clark is a personal acquaintance of the person I am trying to reach out to, it is almost a guarantee that the recipient is going to open the message and see what I have to say about Joe. Obviously I have to follow through on this and mention that Joe gave me a referral or explain how Joe and I have worked together in the past.

Here is another example of an e-mail heading that works:

Subject: McClusky Industries

This is when McClusky Industries is either a competitor of the e-mail recipient or a company otherwise familiar to the person I am trying to contact. Ideally, it should be a company that I have worked with, so I can build my message around the success I had in working with McClusky in the past.

Words and Phrases That Make Strong Subject Lines

Company meeting tomorrow
Your colleague John Jones
Growing your investment portfolio
Beating your quota
10 workplace skills

The Message Text

Now let's turn to the meat of your message. As I indicated earlier, I think e-mails should be short, so you don't have a lot of extra room to play with. Moreover, when constructing your message, you have to do it in a way that takes into account two facts about the way people really read e-mail.

1. Text is inherently boring, and it's more boring as it accumulates. A huge column of text that has an unbroken series of words and sentences will be almost impenetrable to your reader.
2. Human beings are visually driven organisms. They are driven to graphics. And, in the kind of e-mail messages we're talking about, graphics mean bullet points. Bullet points are your secret weapon.

The bullet points in your e-mails should emphasize the key action words you want your recipient to respond to. These action words should tell the prospect what you're going to do for him.

Consider the following message set out with bullet points. Pay attention to the highlighted action words and phrases.

To: Jim Prospect
From: Mike Salesperson
Subject: Upcoming presentation

Jim:

As you requested, here are some thoughts on why it makes sense for me to deliver the proposal in person in front of your regional vice president on May 3. I hope you'll share them with the board.

- For one thing, the RVPs **get a sense of me** as a trainer and see how my **personal style connects** with the material.
- For another thing, **I will be able to demonstrate** the Phone Coach equipment that is a **critical part** of the training program.
- Finally, I will be able to **answer questions on the spot**, rather than putting you in the awkward position of having to check with me and follow up afterward about any queries that they may have about the program content.

Jim, I really think this is the way to go. What would you think of putting me on the agenda for May 3?

Mike

Can you see how each bullet point, through the use of these key words laid out in an attractive visual format, drives home the advantages to be gained in talking to me?

Here's another example:

To: Jane Businesswoman
From: Roger Salesguy
Subject: Appointment tomorrow

Dear Jane:

I want to give you a preview of what I'll be discussing in tomorrow's presentation to your executive team.

- I'll **present the range** of accounting **services** my company offers and **compare** them with our major competitors'.
- I'll offer **projections** of how much **money we can save you** over the next five years through adopting our service.

- I'll **outline the array** of checks and balances in our systems that **ensure their accuracy**.
- I'll **detail the structure** of my proposed working arrangement with your company, as well as **answer any questions** you and your team have.

I want to **confirm** with you that our meeting will begin at 10:00 A.M. and that I should ask for you when I arrive at the building. If you have any **questions or concerns**, please give me a ring at 555-123-5577. **I look forward to speaking with you tomorrow.**

The effect of putting this information in bullet points makes the message forceful, energetic, and easy to get into. The easier your message is to get into, the more eyeballs will actually read it, and the more eyeballs that actually read it, the more fingers will type a response to you and hit "send."

Words and Phrases to Include in the Body of an E-mail Message

I will present
I will outline
detail
demonstrate
facts and figures
spreadsheets
answer your questions
discuss your needs
I look forward to speaking with you

Confirm our appointment
Please contact me

Signatures That Resonate

A major opportunity for spreading the word about your company and its products and services can and should be found at the bottom of every e-mail message you send. This is the portion of the message known as the "signature," and it should be written, revised, and updated as carefully as anything else that appears in your message.

Anyone who must make his or her way through a hundred or so e-mail messages sometimes notices the signature more readily than the body of the message. Why? Because human beings have a tendency to scan to the bottom of a message to see what the point of it is. We want to cut to the chase, so we hit that "Page Down" button or use our mouse to scroll to the very bottom of the message. What this means is that someone who receives a number of messages from us will, over time, receive more exposure to the signature we set up at the bottom of the message than to anything else we write!

It behooves us, then, to create a powerful and compelling signature, and to revise it from time to time so it retains the same basic theme but does not become so familiar that its message fades into oblivion.

Again, words are key here. Just as you would not send out a message to prospects or clients in written form that did not incorporate your company's logo and contact information on a sharp-looking piece of stationery, so you will also want to avoid sending out an e-mail message that contains no reference whatsoever to your company, its website, or your own role within the company.

Of course, there are some important differences between a carefully crafted e-mail signature and a good piece of stationery. For one thing, the stationery is a physical object, and it is an accepted convention to incorporate a logo at some point near its upper left-hand corner. There is no such convention regarding e-mail signatures, primarily because the act of sending an image as part of a logo can set off spam filter alerts.

Here is a model signature to consider adapting:

Stephan Schiffman, President
D.E.I. Franchise Systems, Inc.
www.dei-sales.com
"We Understand Sales"
123 Metropolitan Way
Metropolis, NY 10107
212-555-5555 (office)
212-555-5557 (cell)
212-555-5556 (home)

You read right: That's a home phone number. When I leave a positive impression with a prospect or customer, I want it to be reinforced with accurate information on how to reach me by phone at just about any hour of the night or day.

My signature sends the clear and unequivocal commitment that these people can and should feel free to reach out to me at any one of the three numbers I offer.

I do get a lot of resistance to this from salespeople, and I have told salespeople in training programs that it is a perfectly acceptable alternative to list one's cell phone number and main office number if these are the only two lines that you want to use for business purposes. But supplying the home number sends a message of accountability that is hard to forget.

Remember this, if you remember anything at all about your e-mail message signature: It should send the unspoken message that you wish to be accessible to the other person, and it should offer at least two valid phone options that the person can use to get in contact with you.

The P.S.

When you receive an appeal from the Red Cross or from somebody trying to sell you a new magazine subscription by mail, you virtually always see a P.S. message down at the bottom below the author's signature, whether the document is a single page or longer.

I think the reason that the P.S. message is so powerful in direct mail is that it allows the copywriter to restate all the critical facts of the message and even to issue a call to action. For instance, a P.S. might look like this:

P.S. Call 1-800-999-9999 today to lock in your special low rate of only $12.95 per unit!

The theory is that the person reading the message may drift down to the P.S. or even zip forward to it and read nothing else but that message.

On the whole I think this is an accurate way to look at direct-mail selling, but notice that in our e-mail message we're not trying to close the deal by means of our message. So if we do use a P.S. to restate key points, we want to make sure that we're not doing so in such a way that's going to make the letter likely to be confused with spam.

Feel free to use a P.S. statement at the end of your message to restate a key point and perhaps emphasize the next step you plan to ask for. But make sure that that P.S. is appended to a message that is suitably concise, and be sure you personalize it in such a way that the recipient knows it could only have been addressed to him or her.

Words and Phrases to Use in a P.S.

special offer
Contact us today
one-time
now
Grow your business
profits
product line

Restate When Necessary

One final word of advice about e-mail: When you're replying to a client (or anyone else), don't assume they remember the whole e-mail string. Executives answer a lot of e-mails during the day and have a lot of different conversations. There are multiple priorities, multiple objectives, and multiple contacts to juggle at any given moment. It's a bit much to expect them to keep everything in the front of their minds.

It is therefore incumbent upon you, as a salesperson, to give appropriate context within the body of your message, while keeping the message concise. Offer context that will allow the other person to make sense out of your message even after having had thirty other people interrupt his or her day.

This problem highlights a regrettable disadvantage of e-mail, which is that even though it often *feels* like a conversation to the salesperson, and perhaps even to the person with whom he or she communicating, that "conversation" can be, and often is, interrupted by many other things during the course of the day. So what feels to you, the salesperson, like a small pause may end up feeling to the recipient like a totally different conversation.

Remember, a whole lot can happen between the time you hit "send" at nine o'clock in the morning and the time I read your message at four o'clock that afternoon.

Sample E-mail

Here is a sample e-mail with key words and phrases highlighted.

To: Jane Doe
From: Mary Ann Sailors
Re.   **Grow Your Customer Base by 10%**

Ms. Sailors, I've **worked extensively with companies throughout your industry**. In my fifteen years in this business, I've seen the industry change and develop. **With my help**, companies have been able to:

- **Expand their customer base** by 10–15% in fifteen months
- See **profits** rise by 8–10% in a year
- Develop **internal efficiencies** that save millions

I'd like to **discuss with you** how I can help you **accomplish these goals**. Can we **meet next Tuesday at 10:00** A.M.?
I look forward to talking with you.

Jane Doe
President, ABC Systems
123 High Way
Gotham City, New York 10000
(555) 555-1234 (work)
(554)554-4321 (cell)
(455) 455-2431 (home)
janedoe@abc.com
"Our clients come first!"

CHAPTER 4

Turning Around Common Responses

In this first part of the book we've been focused on your main objective in prospecting: *To get an appointment.* Everything else is subordinate to that. You're not making your pitch yet and you're not trying to close a deal (in truth, you haven't even opened it). All you want is the chance to sit face-to-face with someone in a room.

Of course, not everyone says "yes" when you ask for an appointment. It's important to remember, though, that when someone says, "No, I don't want to see you," it's because that person is responding to you in kind. He or she is responding to the question you posed. Don't think of this as an "objection." Think of it as what it is: a response to what you've just said.

The Four Most Common Responses

You're soon going to realize that virtually every initial "no" response falls into one of these four categories:

1. "No thanks, I'm happy with what I have."
2. "I'm not interested."
3. "I'm too busy."
4. "Send me some literature."

The trick is to learn how to anticipate and handle these responses properly.

"No Thanks, I'm Happy with What I Have"

Earlier I told you that our number one competitor is the status quo. For the most part, people really are happy with what they already have. The vast majority of the people you'll speak to will be happy, relatively "set." Otherwise, *they* would have called *you*. And guess what? They're not calling you!

You don't operate a business that's like a pizza parlor. People don't walk in and talk to you because they want to order something from you. You're reversing the process. You're out on the street, as it were, dragging people in for pizza!

And initially, yes, that person says he or she is happy with what's happening now. In fact, at the moment you call that person, he or she is *already* doing something. In other words, you're interrupting that person when you call.

When a Prospect Gives You Lemons, Make Lemonade

I deal with a lot of banks. In fact, my company works with just about every major financial institution in the United States today. A number of years ago I called a bank at 7:00 A.M. and talked to a senior manager—the type who probably shows up at 4:00 A.M. The conversation went like this:

Steve: Mr. Jones, this is Steve Schiffman from D.E.I. Franchise Systems, Inc. We're a major sales training company here in New York City, and we've worked with . . .

Mr. Jones: Steve, let me stop you right there.

(It's almost as if he held up his hand.)

Mr. Jones: Let me stop you right there. Steve, we're already doing sales training. In fact, today's the first day of the program.

At this point, he held up the telephone so I could hear the noise of the people getting ready for the meeting. There I am at 7:00 A.M., listening to the sound of someone else starting a sales training session. Noise. How do you think I felt?

Mr. Jones: Can you hear? Phil's coming in right now!

I didn't know who Phil was. (I didn't even care who Phil was.) I listened to the noise, as I'd been instructed. Suddenly, it dawned on me. I shouldn't feel bad. I should feel great! This person has just told me he's a potential customer—he does sales training. So without missing a beat, I said:

Steve: You know something, Mr. Jones, **that's great that you're using sales training**. A lot of the **other banks** (and I named several banks that we had worked with) have said the same thing before **they had a chance to see** how our program, especially the cold calling program, would **complement** what they were doing in-house. You know something, **we should get together**. How about next Tuesday at 3:00 P.M.?

(By the way, every word I'd said to Mr. Jones was absolutely true.)

Mr. Jones: (After a pause.) Okay.

I got the appointment.

Think for a moment about how I did that. What words I used. What I said was, in essence, "Other people told me exactly the same thing you did. They had the same reaction you did *before* they had a chance to see how what we do complements (fits into, matches, supports) what they're already doing. We should get together. How about next Tuesday at 3:00 P.M.?"

In other words, I reinforced what Mr. Jones was already doing. I simply said that we could complement what he does, that we fit into that plan, and that we could match that plan. I told him that he should look at our programs *because* of what he's already doing. I didn't tell him how to feel about the situation, or pretend I knew how he felt. I simply told him how I felt ("That's great!"), and then told him the facts.

Don't say, "I sure can understand that," which is the way most people have been taught to turn around responses. It's completely unbelievable. What is there for you to understand at this point in the conversation? Remember: If you speak intelligently with a prospect, the prospect will speak intelligently back to you. People respond in kind. So don't say things like "I know how you feel" or "I can understand that" at this early point in the relationship.

Tell the Truth!

Think again about what I did in the call I just told you about. The bank manager was happy with his current service and I *still* managed to get in the door. Why? Because instead of playing word games, I told him the truth: I'd heard similar reactions from other companies in his industry before they saw how what we offered complemented what they were already doing.

If that's true for you too (and I'm betting it is), then you have a strategy for dealing with the "I'm happy" response.

Words and Phrases to Get Past "I'm Happy with What I Have"

other companies
What we've done for other people
Our service can help
explore
engage
We should get together and talk

"I'm Not Interested"

Let's take a look at the next most common response. Let's say I call someone up and he says to me, "Steve, look, we're really not interested." Has that ever happened to you? Sure. Now here's the big question: Have you ever *sold* to someone who initially wasn't interested? Your answer has to be "yes" because that's what sales is. *Sales is selling to somebody who wasn't interested prior to your call.* Again, if they were "interested," they would have called you.

So here's what I say:

Steve: Well, Mr. Jones, **a lot of people had the same reaction** you did when I first called—before they had a chance to **see how what we do will benefit them**.

Isn't that the truth? Well then, say that. While you're at it, why not tell the person the names of the relevant companies you've worked with? If you have appropriate referrals, you should certainly use them, and this is the perfect time. Tell your contact that the XYZ Company, the ABC Company, and the National Widget Company all had the *same* reaction as him before they had a chance to see how your services could benefit them. It's the truth.

Words and Phrases to Get Past "I'm Not Interested"

help you
benefit you
We've worked with other companies
We've grown profits
Let us show you what we can do
Let us demonstrate our product

"I'm Too Busy"

The third most frequent response is "I'm too busy." In other words, you call somebody and they say, "Steve, I'm too busy. I can't talk now." Typically, salespeople react to that by asking, "Well, what's a better time to call?"

In my seminars, I have plenty of discussions like this:

Salesperson: Steve, I have to leave the program to make a call, because Mr. Jones said to call him at 11:00 A.M.

Steve: Really? Tell you what, we'll take a break and we'll just sit here and wait for you.

Salesperson: Oh, no, I'll be on the phone.

Steve: Trust me. We'll take a break, you'll be back in a minute or two.

Of course, that's exactly what happens. Think about it. Nine times out of ten, Mr. Jones has no reason to sit there and wait until the stroke of eleven for a salesperson to call him.

For Mr. Jones, specifying 11:00 A.M. was a way to get rid of you. That's all it was.

But how do you deal with the prospect who says, "I'm too busy?" There is an effective strategy you can use.

Let's say I call Mr. Jones, and he says that he's too busy to talk. Instead of asking, "What's a better time to call?" I say: **"Mr. Jones, the only reason I was calling was to set an appointment. Would next Tuesday at 3:00 P.M. be okay?"**

Look at what I just did. I took that first response, "Look, I'm too busy to talk," and responded with, "Oh—well, the only reason I was calling was to set up an appointment." After all, you don't really want to have a conversation now! You want to get the appointment. The truth is the other person doesn't want to have a conversation now, either.

Now the prospect generally will not agree to this suggestion. Instead, the prospect will probably raise another of the standard responses we're discussing. For example:

Mr. Jones: Well, I'll tell you the truth. I'm really happy with what I've got.

Now I can go back to the response I've prepared for that kind of statement:

Steve: **Oh, that's great! A lot of people tell me the same thing before they have a chance to see how what we do complements what they're doing.**

Understand: The person hasn't yet said he won't see you. Now you've got another response, and you can deal with that.

Note: Don't try to turn around more than three answers at this point. Instead, you can simply say: "Okay, I'll call you back later." (And mean it!)

Words and Phrases to Get Past "I'm Too Busy"
set up an appointment
Does _____ **work for you?**
How about _____ **?**

"Send Me Some Literature"

This next response is probably the most difficult to handle. This is the person who says to you, "Look, do me a favor. Mail me something." That response is difficult because the premise behind mailing something is that the prospect will look at it, will think about it, and will respond to it intelligently; and then when you call, you'll have an intelligent conversation about it. That's a real problem! Too often, salespeople translate "send literature" this way:

"Well, Mr. Salesperson, I might be interested in what you have to sell. Why don't you send me something. Let me look at it, really study it; then call me. We'll have an intelligent conversation and I, who by that point will have read it all, will let you tell me more about what you offer."

The problem is that 90 percent of all salespeople we surveyed said that their mail somehow never gets through to the person they mailed it to. Obviously that's not correct. Think about it. Your credit card bills, your telephone bill, and your bank statement all get to you. And yet sales material never gets through?

It got through. Your prospects just don't remember it. They don't care about it. They didn't read it. The secretary threw it out. It doesn't really matter what happened to your material, does it? The point is that this approach *doesn't move the sales process forward*. It doesn't get you closer to an appointment.

Here's how to turn that response around. When the prospect says to you, "Look, why don't you mail me something?" Just say, **"Can't we just get together? How about next Tuesday at 3:00 P.M.?"**

It's as simple as that! "Can't we just get together? How about next Tuesday at 3:00 P.M.?" Don't get any fancier than that. If you don't get the appointment, nine times out of ten the person will say, "Well, I'll tell you the truth. I'm pretty happy with what we're doing." And you know how to respond to that!

> ### Words and Phrases to Get Past "Send Me Some Literature"
>
> **Can we get together?**
> **Can I meet with you?**
> **Can we talk at _____?**

Don't Forget to Listen!

Listen to what the other person says. Suppose you hear: "Look, I'm really happy with what I'm doing because I'm using the ABC Widget Company to come in here and work on this."

Now you can say, **"We really *should* get together because of what you're doing. My experience is that we can definitely complement ABC."**

The First Response Isn't Worth Fighting Over

Typically, when you listen carefully, you'll find that the first response isn't really the obstacle it sounds like.

A number of years ago, I called a major bank. This is how the conversation went when I asked a decision maker at the bank for an appointment.

The person said, "Well, I'll tell you the truth. We're really happy with what we've got and everything's okay."

I responded to that by suggesting that what we did could complement what he was already doing.

He said, "Oh, well, the real problem is that we have no budget."

I said, "Well, that's okay, **let's get together anyway.**"

And we got together!

This was the first major sale that I ever made: $75,000.

I was so excited on the drive home that I got a speeding ticket! I learned a very important lesson from that call. What I learned was that the first response had very little validity.

Once I handled the first response properly, the second response emerged.

In other words, responses roll into each other. They're not isolated. Very rarely does anybody simply say "no." People usually say "no," and add a story of some kind: "No, I'm not interested because this is what we're doing now."

My experience is that it's the *second* response that really matters. Once you understand that, you can start to see how well what you're suggesting is going to work. The key is the second response, not the first.

Once you understand this premise, you'll be much more effective in getting appointments. The approach I'm suggesting can be applied to a whole range of potential responses.

I know a salesperson that gets so many appointments it would make your head spin. No matter what a prospect says to her on the phone, she says: "Oh, well, that's okay. Why don't we get together anyway?" Of course, that strategy only makes sense if you use it intelligently and judiciously.

Fighting with a prospect over the first response (or any response, for that matter) is foolish. Often, I ask salespeople, "What do you say when the person on the phone says he's happy with what he has now?" You know how they respond? "Well, Mr. Prospect, I sure could make you happier!" That's a challenge, and a pointless one.

- If the potential client says, "No, we're not interested," many salespeople offer a different equally pointless challenge:

"Well, I don't know exactly what it is that you're not interested in; I haven't told you what I'm calling about yet." Not the best strategy.

- If a potential client says, "I'm too busy to talk," many salespeople, as we've seen, will say, "Well, what's a good time to call you back?" That approach isn't going to work, either.
- If people say, "Send literature," some salespeople respond, "It will only take five minutes. Please, sir, let me come in. I'll get on my hands and knees and I'll do a very quick presentation. If you don't like it, I'll be out in five minutes." I've had salespeople tell me they actually put a watch down in front of the person. "Here's my five minutes," they say, "You let me know when it's up." What foolishness.

You and I are professionals. We should be treated as such. What's more, we need to behave like professionals if we expect to be treated like professionals. The person who's subservient or submissive to the prospective client is not going to be perceived as professional.

Many years ago, I said to a prospective client, "This will only take me five minutes." I'll never forget what happened next. That person said, "Okay, you have five minutes." I went in to the appointment and I started speaking. After five minutes, he stood up and walked out. Foolishness. I created that for myself. But I never will again.

You're a professional. Never forget that as you deal with the responses you hear on the phone.

Sample Objections Scenario

Angela: Hi, Mr. Jones, this is Angela Miracle from LA Industries. We've **worked with DZM Company to raise their profile** in the marketplace and develop a comprehensive marketing plan for them. I'd like to **meet with you to discuss doing something similar** with your company. Does next Friday at 10:00 A.M. work?

Mr. Jones: Hello, Angela. I'm sorry, but we've already got a contract with an external marketing firm, and we're very pleased with the job they're doing for us.

Angela: That's great. **I'm really pleased that you're having a positive marketing experience.** That's not easy to find these days, which is why I'm very excited about what we offer. Our service is comprehensive and has a great industry track record. **When would be a good time** for us to sit down and talk?

Mr. Jones: I'm sorry, Angela, I'm just not interested.

Angela: Well, Mr. Jones, **a lot of people have had that reaction** when I've first spoken to them. But they **learn more about our program** and they're impressed with its **scope, complexity, and its rate of success**. I really do think it would be good for us to talk.

Mr. Jones: I'm too busy just now. My whole afternoon is filled with appointments.

Angela: To tell you the truth, Mr. Jones, **I'm just calling to get an appointment**. We can set one up at a time that's convenient for you.

Mr. Jones: How about if you send me some literature?

Angela: Sure, but let's get together and talk as well. Once you see the **specifics** of what I'm proposing, I think you'll be impressed.

Mr. Jones: Fine. Talk to my assistant, and he'll set something up for you next week.

Angela: That's great, Mr. Jones. I appreciate your time and trouble. Have a great day!

PART II

WHAT TO SAY WHEN YOU'RE INTERVIEWING

Now we're on to the second part of the sales cycle, the one where we try to get as much information as possible from the prospect about her business. If you've done your research beforehand—and you certainly should—some of what she says will come as no surprise. But with the right words and phrases, you can also elicit her insights into her company and industry, and these will provide important ammunition during the presentation and closing phases.

CHAPTER 5

Getting the Interview Going

How will you be able to tell whether you've made it to the interviewing phase? Typically it's when you sit down face-to-face with your prospect for the first time, after having engaged in a few innocuous questions that fall into the "general question" or "small talk" category.

These questions should not take long. I'm personally very suspicious of sales reps that spend a great deal of time in the small talk phase. Some form of initial pleasantry is of course essential, but I think it's important to bear in mind that, as a general rule, we do live in a let's-get-to-the-heart-of-the-matter society.

Some organizations boast a laid-back culture that encourages extensive "give and take" during the initial greetings stage, but it is my opinion that they're easily outnumbered by firms that would rather dispense with the introductions and the small talk relatively quickly and move on to the reason the meeting is taking place. More than one sales rep I've worked with has had the experience of "building rapport" with the key decision maker and getting that decision maker to open up by telling lots of stories, only to be ordered out of the room before anything of consequence happened because the decision maker had another appointment waiting outside that couldn't be changed!

Innocuous introductory or greeting questions, that as we have noted earlier did not fall within the six-category model, might sound like the following examples.

You: **Mr. Jones, how are you?**
Or:
You: **Mr. Jones, it's great to finally meet you. I had a great talk with Alannah outside; is she always that nice?**
Or:

You: **Mr. Jones, nice to meet you. How are things going today?**

These are essentially "getting to know you" questions; they're very nearly content-free, and they serve to cover the initial few moments in which you and the prospect shake hands, remark on the surroundings, discuss the weather, or otherwise acquaint yourself with one another for the first time.

For most of us, the interviewing phase begins in earnest after we step into the prospect's office and we've exchanged a few initial pleasantries. Paradoxically, we must often initiate the interviewing phase at that point of the sale that sounds the most like *we're* being interviewed.

Avoid Talking about Your Product Too Soon

We take a seat, make a little small talk by means of questions like the ones outlined above, and then listen as the prospect says something along these lines:

Prospect: So—what can you do for us?

Or:

Prospect: Tell me about your program.

Or:

Prospect: Let's hear about the way you'd structure a seminar for our salespeople.

Or:

Prospect: Fill me in. I want to hear everything.

These familiar conversation starters, although they're usually delivered with good humor (or perhaps a display of scrupulously maintained patience in the midst of a busy day), are disasters waiting to happen.

Why? The questions the prospect poses sound so inviting and they seem like such great openings that we're usually tempted to tell the person what we can do for him or her. Or we provide all the details of our program. Or we explain the way we'd arrange a seminar for that kind of company we think we're dealing with. Or we explain everything we can think of about our product or service.

For reasons I hope are obvious to you, the prospect's invitation to "tell him about the product," as welcome as it may seem, is one we must politely decline. Actually, to be more accurate, we must replace the question with another one, and we must do it in a way that leaves the prospect feeling good about the shift. Here's what it should sound like:

You: Before we start, Mr. Prospect, would it help **if I told you a bit about me and my company** first?

As you do this, or shortly before you do this, you should extract a notepad and a pen from your briefcase. Even though you're about to give a brief summary about your company, you'll be sending an important visual message by removing that notepad: "I'm here to listen."

Do not ask for permission to take notes. Your aim is to send a nonverbal signal that you are ready to pay attention and ready to do business. The notepad and pen are among the most effective tools a salesperson can employ. In the following pages, we will be talking a great deal about how you can put them to good use.

The simple before-we-get-started question I've just set out is unusual in several respects. For one thing, as the starting point of the interviewing phase, it subtly strips the emphasis from the prospect's typical query about "exactly what do you do" in the current situation to what you and your organization have done in the past. And by the way, in case you were wondering: this inaugural question lays the foundation for all the questions that follow. It does not fall into one of the six categories we discussed earlier in the book, but it is nevertheless mandatory as a starting point.

Posing the above question during the very early part of your postintroduction interaction with the prospect is, in my view, essential. You simply *have* to ask it—that is, assuming you want to get the most you can possibly get from the sales-based interviewing program that is the heart of this book.

If you do, you'll be accomplishing a number of important goals. You'll be letting the prospect know in an unthreatening way that it's time to begin the sales call in earnest. You'll be taking a little pressure off the prospect, who is often uneasy about whose job it is to "conduct" the meeting. And you'll be quietly laying the groundwork for the first real fact-gathering questions you will be asking.

What will the prospect say in response? Well, my experience has been that roughly 90 percent of the time, when you ask . . .

You: Before we start, Mr. Prospect, would it help if I told you a little bit about me and my company first?

. . . the prospect will say something like this:

Prospect: Sure, that sounds like a good idea.

Once in a while, you'll run into a prospect that's in a crisis mode. In such cases, you may get an answer along the following lines:

Prospect: No, I think I'd better outline what we're facing here first.

That's fine. Return to your pad and start taking notes. You will essentially be taking part in an accelerated interviewing stage, one in which the prospect moves several steps ahead. The chapters that follow will show you what to ask and when.

No matter what the prospect says, however, you must avoid going into the specifics of what your organization has to offer the prospect's company. You don't yet have enough information to make any meaningful suggestions.

Let's assume, in the present case, that you're dealing with a standard interview, one in which you've asked the initial question in the way I outlined, and the prospect has told you that he or she has no problem with you briefly summarizing your company's work—and your own. You will proceed to deliver an extremely brief, extremely general accounting of your company's history and some indication of your role in the company. It could sound something like this:

You: I'm the president of RabbWorks, a literary agency, freelance writing service, and packaging firm **that's done work with such publishers as** Prentice Hall, Contemporary Books, McGraw-Hill, and Carol Publishing. We're in our second year of operation, and we're involved in some **extremely exciting projects**, including a book called *The Accelerated Job Search*, which has just been released to the bookstores.

That's about as long and detailed as you should get: two healthy sentences, perhaps three at the most. This biography is not an excuse to discourse at length, show off charts and graphs, or engage in one-upmanship. Keep it short and sweet.

The beauty of this brief statement is that it sounds as though it's about to launch into a hard-sell, but it doesn't last long enough to merit an interruption. Instead, it interrupts itself. And when it interrupts itself, it allows you the first opportunity to use an important questioning technique: framing.

Words and Phrases for the First Phase of the Interview

Can I tell you about my company?
Suppose I give you some background?
Can I talk for a few minutes about what we do?
worked
collaborated
exciting
energizing
boosted profitability
expanded the customer base
improved margins
saw a rise in sales
developed customer service

CHAPTER 6

Six Basic Questions

Before going further, I want to suggest to you that there are six basic questions you should ask in the course of the interview. They relate to the essential things you, as a salesperson, need to find out:

1. What is the customer doing?
2. How is the customer doing it?
3. When and where is the customer doing it?
4. Why is the customer doing it?
5. Who is the customer doing it with?
6. Can you help the customer do it better?

With this in mind, let's look at each of these six questions and what words and phrases we should use to pose each one.

Question Number One: What Do You Do?

Variations on Question Number One are meant to determine the nature of the organization's fundamental business goals or the kind of job the person you're speaking to performs. Even if you believe the prospect is engaged in a business with which you feel you're familiar, the truth of the matter is that—at least at the outset of your relationship—you're not familiar with the unique challenges, opportunities, crises, and compromises that this particular prospect faces on a daily basis. You don't yet know about the organization's history, the typical profiles of its target customers, or the level of success or failure it has achieved in reaching and satisfying those customers. Similarly, you don't yet know about the career path of the particular contact you've hooked up with, his or her position of influence within the organization, or the specific way his or her job relates to the personal and business goals (formal or informal) that we all strive to achieve on some level.

Here are some ways you can ask this question or variations on it:

- **What do you do?**
- **Could you describe your day-to-day operations to me?**
- **What would you say are your basic business objectives?**
- **What are your three most important goals?**
- **What motivates you? What motivates your employees?**
- **How do you handle staff bonuses?**
- **What do you like best about this job?**

Question Number Two: How Do You Do It?

Variations on Question Number Two are meant to determine the means the organization uses to attain its essential business objectives. These questions also serve to cast light on what tactics an individual prospect uses to reach personal goals in a business or career context. Even if you believe the prospect is using a system or service that is similar to those of your other customers, and even if you know that the customer is currently buying a certain product to achieve a particular aim, the truth of the matter is—at least at the beginning of your relationship—you're not familiar with the specific applications or product uses this customer has implemented or rejected. You don't yet know about the organization's past experiments in finding effective ways to attain important objectives. You don't yet know what benchmarks are in place or being contemplated; nor do you know what product-related or system-related successes and failures the organization has experienced. Similarly, you don't yet know about the methods your contact has found (or rejected) when it comes to attaining success or fulfillment on the job. As the relationship with your prospect begins, you do not yet know what broad conclusions his or her company has reached when it comes to determining suitable means for attaining important personal or organizational goals.

Here are some ways you can ask this question or variations on it:

- **Can you give me a general outline of your business plan?**
- **What steps have you taken toward meeting this year's goals?**
- **What are the two top goals for you to accomplish this year?**
- **Can you explain to me how everyone's personal goals fit into the overall goals of the organization?**
- **What makes you uniquely qualified to fulfill your goals?**

Question Number Three: When and Where Do You Do It?

Variations on Question Number Three cover a great deal of ground. They are meant to determine the time frame and physical location of the target organization's operations. Is the business strongly affected by seasonal patterns, or does it operate year-round at essentially the same level? Is a particular element of the business something the company is just introducing, or has it been a mainstay of the organization's operation for some time? Does the organization operate out of a single location, or are there a number of branch offices or satellite facilities? Is the organization highly centralized, with all the initiatives either coming from or subject to the approval of a headquarters office? Or is the target organization a more autonomous unit of a larger operation? Even if the structure, business patterns, and overall business profile of the target company strongly suggest to you that it is similar in all essential respects to existing customers, you must determine the specifics for this unique organization. As your relationship with the new prospect begins, you don't yet know enough about the organization's physical facilities, the timing issues it faces, or the youth or age of the division or company with which you are dealing to draw any conclusions.

Here are some ways you can ask this question or variations on it:

- **What were the reasons you decided to locate your plant/ offices here?**
- **What's your strongest sales season? Your weakest?**
- **What's your key top target demographic?**
- **Could you outline your production schedule for me for the next two months?**
- **What are your target dates for completion of this project?**

Question Number Four: Why Do You Do It That Way?

Variations on Question Number Four are meant to cast a light on the priorities and decision-making process at that target organization, either on the group or individual level. Even if you believe that their decision-making process is substantially similar to that of your other customers, at the outset of your relationship you do not know how the person you're dealing with—or the organization he or she represents—makes decisions. You don't yet know about the organization's formal and informal lines of authority, its corporate culture, or the degree to which the target organization embraces a group-oriented or individualistic style of problem resolution or purchasing. Similarly, you don't yet know about the individual contact's predisposition when it comes to making decisions or approving purchases—if, indeed, he or she is authorized to approve purchases at all.

An important note: When properly asked, many Type Four questions do not sound like direct queries for information on the topic of decision making, authority, or organizational purchasing patterns! They must be constructed and delivered with a certain care and subtlety if they are to yield meaningful information. We'll cover the phrasing of this potentially tricky question category later in the book.

Here are some ways you can ask this question or variations on it:

- **This is a great set of priorities. Was it difficult to set them?**
- **How did you guys come to this decision about production and sales?**
- **Who in the company has responsibility for setting sales quotas?**
- **The decision making here about purchasing is different from what I've encountered at other companies. Could you tell me why it works like that?**
- **Who do you report to in the organization?**

Question Number Five: Who Are You Doing It With?

Variations on Question Number Five are meant to help you determine whether another independent supplier is currently working with your target organization and, if so, which one. Even if you have done extensive library research or personally purchased or used the target organization's product or service, and therefore feel you have a reliable indication as to what vendors the organization is using, you must resolve the issue definitively. For instance, the target organization may have a recent problem with a longstanding vendor and may have severed all ties with them within the last forty-eight hours! Alternatively, an organization about which you have no information could be handling all its work in-house and may not be aware of the advantages (or disadvantages) of working with an outside vendor. As you begin to establish a business relationship with your prospect, you don't yet know the specifics of these issues, and you must! Similarly, you don't yet know about the personal sense of loyalty (or lack thereof) the contact with which you are meeting holds toward a current vendor.

Here are some ways you can ask this question or variations on it:

Have you ever worked with a company such as ours before?

How long have you been working with [competitor]?

Could you outline the services that [competitor] provides you?

What's the thing that [competitor] does for you that most satisfies you? That makes you most unhappy?

Question Number Six: How Can We Help You Do It Better?

Warning! This is an advanced questioning category. It usually should not be posed before you have developed enough information by means of Questions One through Five. Variations on Question Number Six are meant to elicit the organization's or prospect's input in developing your formal proposal or to help finalize the implementation of that proposal. Yes, you read that right: In the best case, you will not write or otherwise dictate the proposal outlining what you can do for the prospect. Your aim is going to be to allow the target organization to become the source of the information you deliver when it comes time to "make a pitch." You're going to do this because winning specific input to the content of your proposal, often through posing Group Six questions, will win buy-in on the part of the prospect, and it will substantially increase the likelihood that the product or service you deliver will meet the organization's specifications exactly. By the same token, you will use Group Six questions to find out how you can build long-term, person-to-person alliances by helping your contact attain the career or performance goals that matter most to him or her. Please note that Group Six questions include questions that, in other programs, might be considered "closing questions." However, these questions are not aggressive, manipulative, or misleading, as typical "get-the-order" questions so often seem to be.

A typical Group Six question designed to finalize the sale is posed only after you and the prospect have worked together to develop a detailed proposal. Such questions typically sound like this: "So what do you think?" or "Where do you think we should go from here?" or "How do you think we should get started?"

Here are some ways you can ask this question or variations on it:

What do you think is the first thing my service could do to help your company?

What are the three most important things you think we should focus on?

What kind of time frame do you see for us accomplishing the target goals in this proposal?

What resources should we provide you?

On a day-by-day basis, who in your company will we be working with most closely?

What's in a Name?

One of the most important advantages of following my six-question model outlined in this chapter is that it avoids the kind of selling that's based on a lie. There are many names for the kind of selling that my six-point model seeks to replace. I call it "need-based" selling, but you'll also find sales trainers who talk about "tactical" selling, or "turnaround-oriented" selling, or selling that "finds the pain," or selling that "focuses on inter-personal keys." There are probably a hundred different variations of the Big Sales Lie that I'm trying to help you eradicate with this program. Whatever you call these many approaches, they are all systems that proceed from the assumption that you know most of the essentials about the prospect from the get-go, and that questioning or interviewing is essentially a tool for establishing some form of control over him or her. That's a critical error, and it's one I have developed the six-point model to help you avoid.

Sample Interview Scenarios

Here are a couple of examples of effective interviewing techniques based on the six-question model. For clarity, I've referenced which questions in the scenarios relate to which questions and their variations.

Example 1

You: . . . which has just been released to the bookstores. Mr. Jones, before I go any further, I'm just curious. **Have you ever met with a book packager before?** [Past-oriented variation on Question Number Five: Who Are You Doing It With?]

Prospect: Yes. We've done a couple of books with Right-Read Associates.

You: Really? **How did working with them go?** [Past-oriented variation on Question Number Two: How Do You Do It?]

Prospect: They had their problems.

You: Is that so? Gee, I've talked to a lot of people who only had positive things to say about them. **What happened?** [Despite the way this question is structured, you actually do know that some of Right-Read's customers are unhappy with them! This is a framed, past-oriented version on Question Number Two: How Do You Do It?]

Prospect: Well, the difficulty was, when it came time to assemble the indexes for the books we signed with them, they claimed that that wasn't covered in their contract. So that was a headache for the production department, and the only way it was resolved . . .

Example 2

You: D.E.I. Management Group is one of the world's premier sales training organizations. We've worked with firms like AT&T, Motorola, and Cigna, and we're currently branching out into international operations, which is pretty exciting. I just concluded a prospecting training session in London last week. Mr. Jones, before I go any further, I'm just curious. **Have you met with a sales training firm or company before?** [Past-oriented variation on Question Number Five: Who Are You Doing It With?]

Prospect: Yes, we have.

You: **What firm did you work with?** [Past-oriented variation on Question Number Five: Who Are You Doing It With?]

Prospect: It's a little outfit known as Capitol Consulting; you've probably never heard of them.

You: No, you're right, I haven't. So **how did the project you were working on with them turn out?** What **kind of issues** did you have to look at? [Past-oriented variation on Question Number Two: How Do You Do It?]

Prospect: I'll tell you the truth, I wasn't too crazy about it. This whole meeting today, actually, I should warn you that it's probably something of a shot in the dark for you because we've basically concluded that sales training really doesn't work for us.

You: Huh. Sounds like you've really had some trouble with this area in the past. So—**is Capitol Consulting an out-of-state firm?** [Framed, past-oriented combination of Question

Number Five: Who Are You Doing It With? and Question Number Three: When and Where Do You Do It?]

Prospect: No, no, it's right here in town. In fact, it's operated by the brother-in-law of our CEO. We've done five or six other programs, and we really haven't been able to track any results in our sales performance whatsoever.

Example 3:

You: Chromium Widgets is the largest manufacturer of specialized widget assemblies in the United States. We've been in business since 1961, and we've developed customized widgets for companies like Pop Fellas Consumer Products, Ideal High Fidelity Manufacturing, and Hopponit Bicycles. Lately we've started to develop widgets solutions for smaller start-up firms, too. Mr. Jones, before I go any further, I'm just curious. **Do you have a relationship with a widget supplier currently?** [Past-oriented variation on Question Number Five: Who Are You Doing It With?]

Prospect: Yes, we're working with Johnell Widget.

You: **So did you have to put up a lot of money up front in order to get things started with them?** I've heard from some of the other people in the industry that a lot of companies sometimes ask for that up-front when they're working with a start-up firm. [Framed, past-oriented variation on Question Number Two: How Do You Do It?]

Prospect: No, actually they put together a pretty flexible payment plan for us, and I guess I'd have to say that was one of the key reasons we went with them. We needed the widgets in a hurry to meet a shipping date we had coming, and when we met with the rep, he talked about one that would let us . . .

CHAPTER 7

The Power of Framing

As you can see from the examples at the end of the previous chapter, you open with a short description of your company: explaining what it does, possibly a little (very little) of its history, and some of its success working with other companies. At the end of this brief biography, you're going to ask a straightforward question regarding the prospect's past use, if any, of the type of product or service you handle. Then you're going to follow up the response you get with a question sequence culminating in a special kind of question, one designed to contradict you. This type of question is known as a framed question, and you'll be using it often.

I should note here that in posing this framed question, you'll be issuing the first honest-to-goodness information-gathering query of your interaction with the prospect, and you'll be beginning the "what happened in the past" portion of your questioning process.

Let me describe exactly what I mean when I talk about a framed question. I realize it sounds a little strange at first to pose a question that's meant to encourage the prospect to contradict you. At a certain point, you're going to incorporate a specific assumption within the question sequence that points in the opposite direction from the answer you "expect."

Go back to the first sample scenario we looked at in Chapter 6.

You: . . . which has just been released to the bookstores. Mr. Jones, before I go any further, I'm just curious. Have you ever met with a book packager before? [Past-oriented variation on Question Number Five: Who Are You Doing It With?]

Prospect: Yes. We've done a couple of books with Right-Read Associates.

You: Really? How did working with them go? [Past-oriented variation on Question Number Two: How Do You Do It?]

Prospect: They had their problems.

You: Is that so? **Gee, I've talked to a lot of people who only had positive things to say about them. What happened?** [Despite the way this question is structured, you actually do know that some of Right-Read's customers are unhappy with them! This is a framed, past-oriented version of Question Number Two: How Do You Do It?]

Prospect: Well, the difficulty was, when it came time to assemble the indexes for the books we signed with them, they claimed that that wasn't covered in their contract. So that was a headache for the production department and the only way it was resolved . . .

Did you notice how the framed question, the one that was designed to get the prospect to correct us, resulted in the prospect offering lots of important information for us to write down on our pad? By the way, if the prospect provides you with the information and you don't write it down, go back three spaces and give $200 worth of Monopoly money to the bank! Writing down the facts shows the prospect that he or she is the most important thing in your universe at that moment in time. That's a good message to leave!

Look Beneath the Surface

By putting forth the assumption—one that we knew was incorrect—that a particular company was easy to work with, we learned that the last book packager with whom this publisher worked tried to win extra payment for developing a book project's index, when the publisher was under the impression that this service was included in the initial contract. Do you think that this unpleasant experience should affect the proposal you develop with this publisher for your next project? Sure it should. In the proposal you eventually work up, you should prominently highlight the fact that the charge includes complete index preparation, executed to the publisher's specifications!

Sometimes the prospect will tell you outright that his previous experience with what you're offering has been a bad one. In the second sample scenario in Chapter 6, the prospect tells the salesperson that sales training simply didn't work for his firm. This reflects any number of discussions I've had with people who've hooked up with poor training outfits in the past. In many cases, rather than finding fault with the company they work with, they conclude that theirs is a specialized line of business, one that really can't benefit from sales training.

In these circumstances, should the salesperson take pity on the prospect's ignorance and inform him of the inaccuracy of his position? Or charge into prosecutor mode and ask him to supply concrete evidence that his industry is somehow different from many others? Should the salesperson pull out a snazzy color brochure filled to the brim with testimonials, and read them word for word just in case the prospect's forgotten how to do that himself? No. All of these approaches will tend to polarize the emerging interpersonal relationship.

Instead, the salesperson poses a question that allows the prospect to indulge his instinct to set the record straight. The salesperson, making a guess that the unknown competitor is a local outfit that hasn't yet established itself, asks the prospect whether the training firm is located out of state. This allows the prospect to correct this—and, in the process, to pass along the critical fact that the "competitor" is in fact a small, and apparently ineffective, firm operated by the CEO's brother-in-law!

Frame Power!

Framing can be adapted to virtually any type of information gap you need to fill. You can use this approach, for example, when you want to learn about who else is bidding on the order you're hoping to land for your company. Instead of asking that question directly ("Who is my competition for this order?"), you simply propose an option that you have good reason to expect the prospect will correct.

Words and Phrases for Framing Questions

Did you have a good experience with [competitor]?
Is [competitor] working out well for you?
Is [competitor] your main supplier?
meeting your needs
up to the challenge
who
what
where
when

Here's another quick example of a framing question that elicits information for you to scribble down on your pad. Remember, you're offering the prospect a chance to demonstrate superior knowledge while at the same time giving you something to work with.

You: So are you working with Plattsburgh Services on quotes for this job? [Present-oriented variation on Question Number Five: Who Are You Doing It With?]

Prospect: Plattsburgh? No, no, they're way too small for a job like this. We've worked up quotes from a few people: Eve Media, Maclen Productions, Business to Business. Those are the people you'll be bidding against.

It Works!

This technique of posing a framed question, one the prospect can feel comfortable correcting, has a distinct advantage over most of the other types of questions you'll see examined in sales programs. It really, truly gets people to tell you what's happened before, what's on their mind at the moment, and/or what they're planning to do in the future.

Just for the sake of thoroughness, let me take a few moments to review the other popular (but not always effective) types of sales questions trainers may have recommended that you use during your early encounters with the prospect.

General Questions

General questions are basically the same structure as the "getting to know you" questions we discussed at the beginning of this chapter. They don't ask for much information, and they usually don't get much. Typical questions in this category sound like: "So how are things?" or "Things still working out okay with the system?" or "How'd you like the new office?" General questions are typically meant to be answered with phrases like "fine," or "okay," and there's a subtle or perhaps not-so-subtle social pressure for your prospect to answer in this way.

Specific Questions

The specific questions are pointed. They don't assume a predetermined answer; they leave the door open for the prospect to give the best response he or she can. The danger with these questions is that they put the prospect on the spot. People aren't great sources of information when they feel threatened. The response you get from a specific question may or may not be accurate, and it may or may not be meaningful. Typical questions from this category sound like this: "Are you the person who handles the decision in this area?" or "If we do X, will your organization do Y?" or "And when will the president of the firm be making his decision?" Specific questions usually seem unthreatening enough to the person phrasing them—they are, after all, simply straightforward requests for information—but they often carry an unintended emotional charge. These are the kinds of questions superiors ask their subordinates. The temptation to bluff or give information that is completely inaccurate is often very strong for prospects who are asked specific questions. Why shouldn't they mislead you? You're not their boss, but you're acting as though you are.

Leading Questions

Leading questions are questions that try to force the prospect into giving a certain predetermined response. This type of question takes great skill to use correctly. Some experienced salespeople manage to use leading questions to highlight problems and determine whether a prospect is likely to buy. Most of the salespeople who engage in leading questions are not highly skilled, however, so the technique is almost universally loathed by the people on the receiving end. Typical questions from this category sound like this: "Are you interested in making a million dollars?" or "Do you care about your family's financial security?" or "Do you care about the level of quality your customers perceive?" When they backfire, which they usually do, leading questions are usually followed by even more irritating specific questions: "Why aren't you interested in making a million dollars?"

The framing technique works consistently and better than any of these approaches, when it's applied correctly. As it turns out, the only sure way to mess up the framing technique is to use it in reverse—to try to get the prospect to "correct" you by making some admission you're bound and determined to yank out, no matter what. In such a case, even though the question is structured as a framing question, it really has more in common with a leading question. If you try to frame questions in this way (by saying, for instance, "After talking to a few of your customers, I was under the impression that your organization wasn't all that interested in improving quality"), you may rest assured that the framing technique will fail spectacularly. You'll come off as arrogant, conceited, and overbearing. And you certainly won't close the sale.

Similar misfires can be expected if you are so uncomfortable with the very notion of admitting that you're wrong that the prospect can sense your anguish when you concede even a minor point. The framed question must arise from a certain humility—humility with poise, to be sure, but humility nonetheless.

There's a price to be paid for getting important sales information from our prospects. We have to check our egos at the door. And that means we have to be willing to make "mistakes" that will result in our being pointed in the right direction by the prospect. It means we have to assume that the prospect's problem is somehow, in some yet-to-be-uncovered way, different from that of the last person with whom we've spoken. It means we can't be intimidated by the idea of being corrected or fearful of posing a question because we think it may expose a gap in our knowledge base. The whole point is to expose as many gaps as possible in our knowledge and then get the prospect to help us fill them.

If we already knew the answers about this prospect's situation, we wouldn't have to listen. But we don't know all the answers, so we do have to listen. In short, we have to give up the instinct that we're always right. And we have to demonstrate that we're willing to be righted.

We're not *Jeopardy!* contestants, rewarded for every correct response that happens to be phrased in the form of a question. We're not taking time out of the prospect's busy day in order to show how smart we are. We are facilitators, professional connectors of problems to solutions. Just as a consultant or a doctor or an interior specialist must gather as much information as possible about the situation at hand before formulating a plan of action, we must do the same.

A Dream Come True?

This method of eliciting information is often a tricky undertaking because there are times in the sales rep's day-to-day work when the prospect appears simply to volunteer all the necessary information. However, those volunteering episodes can be deceptive encounters. If you simply nod and point the person toward one of your solutions, you'll probably get a sale. But you won't build a partnership. Those instances of sublime prospect cooperation, those times when it seems we can do no wrong—when it seems, in fact, that we don't have to do anything in order to close the sale—all those dream-come-true exchanges are almost always traps.

You read that right. Even though you get the sale, those kinds of interactions with prospects typically represent short-term alliances at best. In the long term, these situations are traps in which you are basically invited to warm up the prospect for an eventual alliance with one of your competitors. If you consistently fall for the trap, you won't dig into the prospect's history, as the three framed questioning dialogues we saw did, and you'll probably perform, over time, at the bronze medal level. If every once in a while you work up the courage to ask the kinds of framed questions we've just seen when a sale "falls into your lap," you'll sometimes get the key information you need, and you'll likely end up performing at a silver medal level over time. To perform at the gold medal level, however, you must commit to asking the right questions in the right manner all the time.

You have to be willing to ask. You have to be willing to let the prospect take the lead in responding. And you have to be willing to be corrected.

Beware of the Ritual Responses!

Let me make one more important general point on questioning. Some of the dominant patterns in the American language and culture in general, and in American business language and culture in particular, make our questioning work harder. As a brief description of initial pleasantries that appeared earlier in this chapter reflects, we live in a country in which questions like "How are you?" and "How's business?" are typically seen as ritualistic conversation openers. As a general rule, they're not seen as honest-to-goodness requests for information.

When was the last time you picked up the phone and responded to someone's "How are you?" query by actually telling them, in detail, about your current emotional state? Foreigners who conduct business with our companies often complain that Americans are insincere and that we "ask how people are but don't want to hear the answer."

For most of us—particularly men—there is a tendency to shut down when we hear, or phrase, questions at the outset of an exchange with a stranger. It's very easy for people to go into "default mode" and assume that the first few questions of any meeting are basically innocuous, no matter how they're structured. This means that it is incumbent on you to deliver your first question—the one at the end of your company biography, the one I preface with the phrase "I'm just curious"—very carefully indeed. You must deliver this question with the utmost sincerity, and you must make it clear that you are asking because you are interested in hearing the prospect's response. You don't want to have to answer your way out of an exchange like this:

You: . . . which has just been released to bookstores. Mr. Jones, before I go any further, I'm just curious. Have you ever met with a book packager before? [Past-oriented variation on Question Number Five: Who Are You Doing It With?]

Prospect: Oh, we met with a lot of people, yeah, in all different categories, all different levels. Lots of different people, authors, agents, you name it. Hey, can I get you a cup of coffee?

If you follow the advice I offered a little earlier in this chapter and actually open up your notepad and be prepared to take notes on this initial question, you will virtually eliminate the possibility of your prospect shutting down on you in this way.

Sample Framing Question Scenario

Before leaving this topic, let's take one more look at how to ask framing questions and the kind of responses they might elicit.

You: I understand that **you guys have been working for a couple of years with** XYZ Corporation as your main shipping vendor.

Mr. Jones: Well, we did until last year when we shifted to the ABC Company.

You: Really? I'm surprised you made that shift after so many years with XYZ. **Could you tell me the reason for the shift?**

Mr. Jones: We felt that we weren't getting the kind of personalized attention we'd had during the earlier years of the contract. And they were late with some significant shipments and didn't really take a strong, proactive role in fixing the problem.

You: **So now ABC has addressed those issues?**

Mr. Jones: Well, no. To tell you the truth, we're not very happy with them either. They've missed some items on shipments, and like the XYZ Corporation, they haven't been as energetic as we'd like in fixing the problem . . .

CHAPTER 8

Finding Out about the Past and Future

At this stage, you need to explore the history of your prospect's company, which is the essential first part of assembling a comprehensive portfolio of information about the organization. But the first order of business in developing that information is one you might not expect. Before you can talk about the company's past, you must ask your prospect briefly about the target organization's future plans.

Why? Because there's absolutely no point in wasting your time—or the prospect's, for that matter—if your prospecting work has pointed you toward the right organization but the wrong person. If you haven't hooked up with the right person, you need to know that. And by the "right person," I mean either the official decision maker who can say "yes" to what you have to offer or the appropriately placed insider who is in a position to lobby that official decision maker on your behalf. Both of these people, by definition, have some idea of what the organization's future plans are in the area of your product or services. That's why the early part of your inquiry into the organization's past is marked by a question that explores how much your contact knows about future plans.

Of course, you've already asked your prospect something about the past. In the last chapter, we saw how you interrupted your own company's biographical statement with a question about the target company's past meetings with competitors or past use of products or services that parallel yours. (By the way, if it seems appropriate, you can point that question toward whether the target organization ever considered using your product or service in the first place.)

The initial question forms a natural—and, I would argue, indispensable—bridge to a question about the future.

If your prospect seems to display a general ignorance about what's happened in the past with regard to the use of your product or service, there's a pretty good chance that he or she is not the person you should be talking to. Or, at any rate, he or she is not the only person you should be talking to. If your prospect has little or no idea what the plans are for incorporating (or not incorporating!) your product or service in the future, guess what? There's no doubt. You need to find a way to hook up with someone else in the organization. There's no point asking this person anything about the company's past. All you're going to get in response is a lot of silence or, worse yet, inaccurate information.

Your game with the second honest-to-goodness question of the session, then, is to find out how much your prospect knows about the future plans of the organization in the area under discussion. If the person you're after gives you a meaningful, informed response, of course you're going to take it all down on your notepad.

> ## Words and Phrases to Find Out about the Past and Future
>
> **What are you trying to do?**
> **Where is the company going?**
> **What services/products are you developing?**
> **in progress**
> **over the horizon**
> **one/five/ten years out**
> **projections**
> **forecasts**

anticipate
accomplish
complete

Here are some examples of what the second question—the one about the future—would sound like:

You: Tell me—what's the main thing **you're hoping to make happen next quarter** with the widget project we talked about on the phone? [Future-oriented variation on Question Number One: What Do You Do?]

Or:

You: Here's something I'm wondering. What kinds of relationships **are you hoping to develop in the future** with regard to freelance manuscript development services or book packaging providers? [Future-oriented variation on Question Number One: What Do You Do?]

Or:

You: What are your plans for sales training **for the next year or two**? [Future-oriented variation on Question Number One: What Do You Do?]

Or:

You: What areas do you **anticipate** trying to focus on with your project acquisition next year? [Future-oriented variation on Question Number One: What Do You Do?]

Or:

You: Can I ask you something? What are you **trying to get accomplished** in this area? [Future-oriented variation on Question Number One: What Do You Do?]

The last question is one of my favorites, by the way. It's informal, doesn't presume a high degree of technical knowledge (important, since many top decision makers don't possess a great deal of technical knowledge), and it's pretty close to being unerringly accurate at flushing out people who aren't in the loop. People who can't help you get closer to a sale simply don't know what to do with the question, and any attempt they make to fake their way through it is usually immediately obvious.

If the person you're talking to seems to have some idea what's going on with regard to your product or service in the future, or appears to have a strong sense of what's happened in the past, or gives you the general impression of being able to influence matters in one direction or another (even without saying so directly), then you should proceed with the interview.

If, on the other hand, the person you're talking to gives every indication of being a tangential player, as evidenced in the exchange like this:

You: So, Mr. Jones, let me ask you. Is the company **planning to stay with a work force** that's roughly the same size over the next twenty-four months?

Or:

Does your organization **anticipate** doing any on-site training during the **next fiscal year**?

Or:

How many new widget programs is your work group **planning to be involved** with next quarter? [Future-oriented variation on Question Number One: What Do You Do?]

Prospect: Gee, I really couldn't tell you.

Or:

You know what? That's a good question!

Or:

Is that really important?

You need to say something like this:

You: Hmm. Well, this is kind of **important**, and let me tell you why. We've found a lot of clients have learned that they were tied to a program that had them paying more than they had to for the service (Or: losing customers, missing revenue opportunities, etc.) because we weren't able to work with them to **forecast** what they were going to do in this area. So **it really can make a big difference** for your organization. Do you know **who we could talk to that could point us toward your company's plans** in this area?

In other words, you're going to work with your current contact to help resolve a pressing business problem, and you're offering that person the opportunity to help present the solution to the problem. You're not going to abandon your current contact just because you have concluded that he or she seems unlikely to be in the loop on purchase decisions; instead, you're going to try to turn him or her into a business ally as you work your way through the organization. You're going to make an unspoken offer to turn your current contact into a hero by letting him or her be the one who can bring your solution to the attention of the people who make decisions in your area.

Why Not Just Ask?

You may be wondering: Why can't I just ask whether the person I'm talking to is the decision maker? That certainly seems as though it would be the most straightforward approach, doesn't it? After all, it's not as though you're discussing state secrets here. Either the person you're talking to handles decisions in this area or the person you're talking to doesn't.

There's a problem, though. During the early parts of the sales cycle, people don't mind in the least lying to you on this point. I'm sure it's all very innocent. I'm sure that over the years prospects have assembled a whole collection of great excuses for lying to salespeople when it comes to answering this question. But it is an inescapable fact of sales life that prospects do lie when asked about their status as the decision maker. My own experience leads me to believe that roughly half of all prospects asked this question will give an inaccurate, misleading, or deceptive response. This means every other time you ask the question, you're getting bad information. You might as well toss a coin.

If you stop and think about it, this state of affairs actually makes sense from a certain angle. Most of us like to impress other people, and few of us, all things being equal, are going to de-emphasize our importance to the organization we work for. Therefore, people who aren't involved in a certain business decision have an interest in leading you to believe that they are involved in that decision.

On the other hand, people like to be able to make important business decisions—whether on their own or with others in the organization—in a secluded, distraction-free environment. For better or worse, thanks to the efforts of the many find-the-need salespeople out there, many businesspeople today have come to the understandable and probably accurate conclusion that most salespeople are distractions. They assume, at first, that you're like all the rest of the salespeople they've spoken to. So, instead of trying to convince you they really are in the loop, some people have an interest in leading you to believe that they aren't involved in making the decision.

Here's another way to look at it. Many prospects think to themselves, "Hey, you may or may not be working with us, so who cares whether I tell you the truth now?"

In the final analysis, the underlying reasons for this information gap aren't as important as our acceptance of the fact that the gap exists. If you're honest with yourself, you'll probably have to admit that your own experience has shown that simply asking the prospect "Are you the decision maker in this area?" is a colossal waste of time, and a great way to find yourself chasing down blind alleys.

Determining whether the prospect knows about future plans affecting your product or service, on the other hand, is an extremely reliable indicator of whether the prospect is involved at some level with the decisions that will affect you. So use your second question of the session as I've suggested here. Together with the answer to the first question about the company's history, the two answers you receive will tell you a lot about who you're dealing with and where they're situated in the network of authority that hands down the "buy/don't buy" judgments.

The way your contact responds to those two questions is usually enough to give you a sense of where to go next—usually, but not always. If the pair of questions I've outlined here doesn't do the trick, and you still feel uncertain about exactly who you're talking to, there is one more avenue open to you. It must, however, be undertaken with great attention and care.

The Last Resort

The "last resort" query we're about to look at is basically a variation on the most advanced of the six sales questions, Question

Number Six. This is a dangerous question and one that, if mishandled, can scuttle the sale for you! So please be sure to deliver it exactly as I outline it.

The key to getting away with this question, which aims directly at finding out who in the organization is involved with making purchase decisions, is not making eye contact during the second half of the question. For some reason, looking the person directly in the eye when you pose this question is almost always perceived as a challenge. So, instead of looking the prospect in the eye for the whole question, you're going to look down at your notepad halfway through the sentence and simply await the information the prospect's about to pass on to you. This is an extremely important step—if you ask this Group Six question at this stage, early in the interviewing phase, you must follow this advice if you hope to keep the sales cycle moving forward.

Here's what the question looks like:

You (while looking at the prospect): Mr. Jones, let me ask you this. **Who in** . . . (Look down to your notepad and hold your pen in your hand as though you're awaiting instructions) **. . . the organization would be involved in making the decision to work with us on a project like this?** [Future-oriented variation on Question Number Six: How Can We Help You Do It Better?]

Note that this question does not ask the prospect directly whether he or she is involved in the decision-making process. Nor does it attempt to close the sale. It simply requests information and then sits on a nice fat silence, which is what you should expect to hear when you pose it. No matter how long that silence lasts, keep staring at your pad and wait for the prospect to respond. When he or she does, write down what you hear and proceed accordingly. If you conclude that you do in fact need to reach someone else in the organization, return to the ally-building technique that we just outlined, and try to get your prospect to steer you in the right direction.

Once again: In moving forward to the variation on Question Number Six at this stage of the relationship, you must take great care not to intimidate the prospect, polarize the relationship, or offer any excuse to pass along any faulty information. Break off eye contact as I suggested, and keep your focus on your notepad until you hear the information you need.

Let me be clear, too, on this point: Your aim here is not to march lockstep through the organization until you find yourself sitting across the table from the one, the only Big Kahuna, the person who carries sole and exclusive responsibility for deciding whether to buy from you. Reaching that person is nice when it happens, but you can't make obtaining a face-to-face meeting with that individual your objective at this stage. There are a number of reasons for this, the most important of which being that there may not be such a person in the first place.

At many organizations (mine, for instance), the so-called "decision-making authority" on key purchase decisions is diffused among a number of people. There may be one person (or one committee) in charge of researching issues and developing a recommendation, and another person who will almost certainly approve that recommendation but who will nevertheless review it closely before a purchase order is issued. Such ad hoc arrangements are the way the real business world operates, and these arrangements often don't reflect formal titles or organizational outlines.

So don't be misled by titles or flowcharts. For one thing, titles can be extremely deceptive; a contact can have the most impressive title in the world, but have literally no knowledge in the area that title points toward. Titles and hierarchical arrangements aren't the point. Your objective is not to track down the person who can say "yes"; although you should certainly take the opportunity to meet with that person if you find him or her! In most cases, however, your aim is simply to hook up with an insider: someone who knows exactly what the decision process is going to be and who is likely to be able to work on your behalf as it goes forward.

CHAPTER 9

The Art of Small Talk (That Isn't Small)

Let's assume that you used the techniques outlined in the previous chapter and that you've found your way to the right person. Your aim now is to find out as much as you can about the company's history as it affects your product or service, right?

Well . . . it can be. I believe, however, that it's usually just as important to find out about your individual prospect's past. After all, when it comes right down to it, you're not really selling to a company at all. You're selling to another person, a person with a career to think about and a daily series of problems to address, just like you. Depending on the situation, once you've satisfied yourself that you're dealing with the right person, you may decide to start asking a few questions about the person sitting across the desk from you.

Now, you know and I know that sales calls don't follow a predetermined script. In fact, the whole idea of this book is to give you the verbal tools to think on your feet. Sometimes, the second you walk in the door you have a pretty good idea what position the prospect occupies in the organization. And sometimes you don't. When you feel confident enough about the nature and scope of your prospect's job to alter the basic pattern a little bit—this may happen as a result of information you developed during your cold call, or information you received from the third party, or something you read in a newspaper or trade magazine—you may decide that the initial "small talk" phase of your visit presents you with a perfect opportunity to find out a little more about your prospect's mindset, typical approach to dealing with problems, and career aspirations.

There are a series of "small talk" questions you can ask during the initial greeting-and-pleasantry stage that will help you do just that. I should point out that my own preference is to use these questions only when I'm relatively certain that I'm dealing with someone who is in a position to help me move the sales cycle forward. The reason? Well, people love to talk about themselves, and they love to do so at length. Issuing an invitation to hold forth on one's history, current projects, and future plans often results in some long speeches. When those long speeches come from someone with whom I'm hoping to build a long-term business alliance, I'm happy to take it all in. If I don't know whether I'm talking to the person who schedules sales training or the person who sorts the mail in the morning, I tend to be a little more conservative about the way I spend my time, since it's the single most important asset at my disposal. That's my decision; you may come down differently on this issue.

In any event, if you decide to do so, you can use the initial meet-and-greet phase of your meeting to get your prospect to open up about personal rather than organizational aims, predispositions, and past experiences. The beauty of doing so is that the questions you'll use do just as good a job of managing the social niceties, which are so essential to a first-time business meeting, as anything you can say about the weather, the prospect's office, or an upcoming holiday weekend. Of course, you can also introduce these questions at later points in the interviewing phase, but my experience has been that when delivered briefly and with full attention during the small talk phase, these kinds of questions can help you develop a real, lasting rapport with the decision maker that makes all the subsequent work a great deal easier. Nevertheless, I know of a good many salespeople who use these prospect-oriented questions as backups; they appeal to this line of questioning when they feel their main line of questioning isn't going as well as it should. That's certainly a workable strategy, too.

Words and Phrases for Making "Small Talk"

How long have you been with the company?
Where were you before that?
Where in the company did you start?
How were you hired?
Who was your first boss?
How'd you hear about the company?
where
when
how
who

Here are examples that will demonstrate what "small talk that isn't small talk" questions can sound like.

Example 1

You: This is a great office. **How long have you had this job?** [Personalized, past-oriented variation on Question Number Three: When and Where Do You Do It?]

Prospect: Oh, gee, let's see—it must be six years now.

You: Really? **How did you get it?** [Personalized, past-oriented variation on Question Number Two: How Do You Do It?]

Prospect: Well, it was sort of an odd combination of coincidences. An old friend of mine I used to work with got a better job here, and mentioned to the boss that I was closing down my consulting firm . . .

Example 2

You: I'm just curious—**how long have you been with the company?** [Personalized, past-oriented variation on Question Number Three: When and Where Do You Do It?]

Prospect: Well, I think it's four years now.

You: No kidding. **How did you get hired?** [Personalized, past-oriented variation on Question Number Two: How Do You Do It?]

Prospect: Tell you the truth, it was a temp assignment, but they liked what I did during crunch time so much that they asked me if I'd consider coming on full-time. The first job I held was as accounting clerk, but that only lasted about six months; after that I was moved up to . . .

Example 3

You: Boy, this is a really exciting company. **How did you get started here?** [Personalized, past-oriented variation on Question Number Two: How Do You Do It?]

Prospect: I was here when they started the place up.

You: Wow!

Prospect: Yeah, I was one of the people Mike called when he wanted to get things going. We didn't really have much in the way of job titles back then; I guess you could have called me the sales manager. All that meant back then was I was the one who'd hire the salespeople and talked to them every day, but a lot of the time it also meant I got to pick up the phone and dial the numbers when it came to reaching new customers . . .

These are all, of course, questions that point toward the prospect's past, questions that encourage the person to fill in the points as he or she sees fit. Asked with sincerity, the questions serve as tangible proof that you're interested in your conversational partner. Delivered correctly with genuine feeling, these questions can be extremely flattering. They can also be remarkably effective at getting people to open up to you. They may result in some extended monologues and, not infrequently, unsolicited lectures on career enhancement, corporate strategy, and industry trends. Those lectures, which can often fall into the "long-winded" category, are the reason I try to reserve these types of questions for people I'm already fairly certain will be somehow involved in the sales cycle. They're the people I want to spend most of my time finding out about.

Learning from the Answers

The answers you receive to these types of questions will also tell you a good deal about the prospect's way of approaching problems, level of education, and degree of experience in dealing with vendors other than a main supplier. Listen not only for the hard facts but also for the direction from which the prospect approaches key issues. If your contact remarks that he got his job as a result of his ability to "put out fires," and goes on to note that he spends most of his time handling issues of "crisis resolution," there's a good chance that to a large extent he views his job as a series of opportunities to save the day for the company . . . typically by addressing problems someone else missed early on. As you work together to develop your proposal, you'll probably want to formulate your solutions in a way that emphasizes dramatic settlements of potentially catastrophic oversights—with that credit accruing to your prospect, of course.

Be sure to listen actively (a topic covered in the next chapter). This is where showing interest in and involvement with your prospect's story can really pay off. Properly handled, this phase of the interview offers a goldmine of information about the company and the prospect.

Past-oriented questions, those on the personal level, will also tell you something about the prospect's personal familiarity with your type of product or service. Resist at all costs any temptation to display how your knowledge exceeds the prospect's. This is a dangerous maneuver in virtually any situation; in certain cases, it can be downright suicidal.

Let's assume that your initial "small talk" questions point out your prospect's inexperience in dealing with other vendors. This is a common state of affairs, especially when the organization is making the transition from a smaller, entrepreneurially oriented company to a larger company in which decision making is, of necessity, somewhat more decentralized. In such companies, the entrepreneur who started the company has only recently relinquished control of purchase decisions, and he has probably only done so after an extended period in which he tried to run the whole show himself. Often, the entrepreneur will select someone who has been with the company for some time to make purchase decisions in the area in question. Unfortunately, the entrepreneur will likely have remained with a single vendor for so long that the company has no practical knowledge of what else is on the market. (A similar pattern often occurs in larger companies that pride themselves on "promoting from within," and as a result develop staffs that haven't even thought seriously about switching vendors for the past ten years or so.) In such situations, the new decision maker, wary of making a high-profile mistake, may adopt an extremely cautious it's-always-worked-this-way-for-us approach—especially if such an approach is in keeping with the founder's line of thinking in your product or service area. When you encounter a situation like this one, beware. Flaunting your superior knowledge and your vast array of past projects in front of the terrified person whose job it is to decide whether to switch vendors may only serve to intimidate them.

These decision makers are usually looking for a vendor who offers a single significant advantage over the existing product or service provider, but who strongly resembles the current vendor in other respects!

Ask about Her Career

Finally, even though they don't directly ask the prospect to talk about future plans, past-oriented questions that focus on your prospect's career will begin to give you some idea of the contact's promises and aspirations. You'll get a sense of how happy your prospect is in the job, the main contribution he or she makes to the organization, and what level of enthusiasm accompanies discussions of the person's work. These can be critically important factors.

I once met with a prospect who had agreed, somewhat reluctantly, to discuss his company's sales training plans. When it came time to head to his office for the meeting, I knew from a little outside research that the man with whom I would be meeting had personally decided all training-related purchasing issues for this firm for some time. As a result, I felt comfortable incorporating small-talk-that-isn't-small-talk questions during the early part of our meeting.

I walked in. I told him it was great to meet him. I complimented the office. I mentioned what the traffic had been like. I smiled. Each of these innocuous conversational "openers" produced the same result from my prospect: a forced smile and a low grunt of agreement. He motioned to a seat and took his own place behind his desk.

After taking a seat, I decided to use the how-did-you-get-started questions sequence right away, in order to try to shed some light on exactly what kind of mindset I was dealing with.

"Gee, Mr. Smith," I began, "I guess you know this is a very highly respected company. You've got a great job. How long have you been with the company?"

"Twenty-seven years," Mr. Smith responded.

"Ah," I responded. And before I could pose the follow-up, Mr. Smith decided he needed to elaborate on the answer. "Twenty-seven years and two months," he went on.

"I see," I said.

"Twenty-seven years, two months, nineteen days, and one hour," Mr. Smith concluded. I thought perhaps he wanted to break the time down into minutes and seconds so I waited. But the fellow just looked at me with a little grin on his face, so I kept going.

"How do you like the job?" I asked.

"Used to love it. Now I can't stand it," he answered. "I'm going to retire soon."

"No kidding," I responded. "When are you planning to retire?"

Mr. Smith's smile got a little broader. "Four months, eleven days, and seven hours from now. Only thing I'm interested in right now is closing the doors and sealing my boxes. Any other questions?"

"No," I answered, "I think we've about covered it. Thanks for taking the time to get together with me today. You have a nice day."

"You're welcome," he said politely. "You too."

There was no way I was going to get any meaningful information, much less the beginnings of a long-term relationship, out of Mr. Smith. His focus was on getting out the door. And that was totally understandable. Talking any further about his sales training needs would have been a complete waste of his time . . . and mine. I shook his hand, left his office, and, outside the building, made a note in my calendar to check back for another appointment with Mr. Smith's successor on the day after the retirement date that was now etched so clearly in my mind.

Four months and twelve days later, I made an appointment—and I eventually closed that sale.

What Else Can You Do with Small Talk?

Many of the salespeople I work with decide to explore not only the prospect's past but also his current projects and future goals during the initial "small talk" phase of the meeting. I agree with this approach as long as it isn't pursued mindlessly. You, the salesperson, are usually the best judge of how much emphasis to place on questions directed toward the prospect's, rather than the organization's, viewpoint, and how many of these questions to ask. Because they can be (and often are) asked during the meet-and-greet phase that precedes your description of what your company does, let's look at some examples of questions that ask the prospect to share his present activities and future plans with you. As we do, however, please understand that you are free to incorporate the questioning techniques that follow at the other points of the interviewing phase as well.

Words and Phrases to Use in Small Talk

What are you doing now?
What plans do you have for next year?
What's exciting on your horizon?
What projects do you anticipate working on?
Where will you be in five years?
planning
changing
anticipating
exciting
stimulating
expanding
increasing responsibilities
growing scope

Note that in many of the examples that follow, when you ask about the person, you will automatically and quite naturally be asking about the organization, too.

Example 1

You: So it sounds like there's been some major **change of focus** in the last year around here. **How does that affect what you're doing here?** I mean, is this job something that's **evolving** to meet all these new demands, or is it pretty much settled in terms of the outlines of what you do? [Personalized variation on Question Number One: What Do You Do?]

Prospect: Well, I met with the VP of finance in February, and we decided to work through some important changes in the job description, based on all the organizational changes that had been happening since the merger. So, yes, I'm in kind of a transitional phase. We're working to get me focused less on the day-to-day number-crunching stuff and more on the ways I can help streamline operations and eliminate some of the duplication you expect to find when two companies turn into one company.

You: But it sounds as though that's not exactly an overnight process.

Prospect: It certainly isn't. I mean, I have a lot of organizational commitments that I'm in the process of handing off to other people and other departments. And I can't simply stop paying attention to that. People still need to get sales reports, still need to find out how many customer service people are dealing with what product and why. So it's sort of a balancing act right now.

Example 2

You: So what kinds of projects are **you personally handling now**? [Personalized variation on Question Number One: What Do You Do?]

Prospect: Me, I'm basically in charge of all the company seminars and training sessions, and we put together between twelve and fourteen of those a year. This year, we're budgeting to mount fourteen training sessions.

You: Well, that's quite a schedule. **How do you usually determine** what the topics are going to be? [Personalized variation on Question Number Four: Why Do You Do It That Way?] (Note: Group Four questions can address the means by which a person or individual makes decisions and are often phrased indirectly.)

Prospect: That's something I discuss with the CEO. He and I sit down for a meeting at the beginning of the year and we set up the broad outline of what we want to work on. Then we review that quarterly and make any changes that seem appropriate.

You: So you're pretty much getting this from the horse's mouth.

Prospect: Oh, yes. This is Mr. Stone sitting down with me in a room, the two of us figuring out what we want to work on.

You: Okay. That's **good to know**. Now, when you set up these seminars, do you typically try to find someone from the outside to work with, or **do you develop all the material** in-house? [Variation on Question Number Five: Who Are You Doing It With?]

Prospect: I set up about 60 to 70 percent of the programs myself. I mean, I personally write the text and set up the manuals, after meeting with the appropriate internal people. And the remainder of the training is something we coordinate with outside vendors.

You: And you conduct the training right here? [Variation on Question Number Three: When and Where Do You Do It?]

Prospect: Yes, right here. Both for things we've developed in-house and for programs, we do all the training right on-site in this facility. That's very important to Mr. Stone. On the in-house material, I usually handle the presentations on my own.

Example 3

You: **So where do you hope this job leads you? What do you want to be doing five or six years from now?** [Future-oriented variation on Question Number One: What Do You Do?]

Prospect: You know, that's an interesting question. I guess I'd have to say I'm hoping I could continue to grow here at the company. I mean, I like the location, the industry is one I feel I've got a real proficiency for, and I've spent most of my career here.

Adapting to a new set of situations could be tricky, so I've always thought about working toward a vice-president position here; something that would continue to make the most of my abilities and still challenge me. But I need to sign some fairly big books, hopefully something in the personal finance area, before I can think about making a move like that.

Example 4

You: **So where do you hope this job leads you? What do you want to be doing five or six years from now?** [Future-oriented variation on Question Number One: What Do You Do?]

Prospect: It's hard to say. To tell the truth, I've been feeling a little stifled here the last year or so. Who knows where things are going to go, you know? I guess you make the best of things you can. Anyway—let's talk business.

You: Okay, sure. Do you mind if I ask—**who's involved in making the final decisions** with regard to this training budget we'd be working with? [Variation on Question Number Six: How Can We Help You Do It Better?] *Warning!* This question must be executed properly. See the earlier notes on the proper use of your notepad. Do not make direct eye contact with the prospect during the main part of the question.

Prospect: Well, technically, Jane and I handle that, but you should probably be talking to Allison about some of these issues as well.

You may feel a little skeptical that prospects will actually hold forth on such issues as long-term career planning for you. Don't be. The seductive power of full attention is a remarkable advantage in the sales world. Every time I watch it in action, I'm amazed that salespeople don't make better use of it.

Make It Easy to Talk to You

The kinds of discussions we look at do happen quite naturally when you stick to the six basic categories. When you phrase your questions in a nonthreatening fashion and then truly listen to the responses your prospective offers, you can get hold of some essential intelligence. In the last exchange, for example, we learned that our prospect is probably a little restless in her current job. She gave us a couple of nod-and-a-wink indications that she may not be long for this particular company. She tactfully changed the subject when it appeared that she might have gone too far. And then when we followed up on the uneasiness by attempting to confirm, via the "I'm just staring at the notepad" technique, exactly who would be involved in making the decisions, she confidently pointed us toward someone who did have formal authority in our area. Could Allison be in a position to take over some of our prospect's responsibilities in the months to come? Who knows, but we've been pointed in Allison's direction.

These kinds of exchanges—the ones that clue us in on personal intentions that usually remain buried below several layers of business formality—are only possible when we truly pay attention to the prospect and make it clear to him or her that we're interested in becoming an ally. Purposeful, tactful questions, along the lines of the ones we've just seen, are superb tools for doing just that.

More Questions to Ask about the Past

So much for the "small talk" that can carry big implications for your emerging relationship with the prospect. Let's look now at some of the other ways you can formulate questions about the organization's history during the interview phase.

Please bear in mind as we examine these questions that you do not have to pose them all during your first face-to-face meeting with the prospect.

During some meetings, of course, things will be going so well, and you have so much time at your disposal that you'll be in a position to query the prospect in great detail about what has happened in the past during a single meeting. (You'll also be able to use the material and subsequent chapters to find out all you need to know about what the company's current operations look like, as well as what future plans are in the works.) At other meetings, however, either you or the prospect will want to cut things short for some reason, and you'll agree to get together to follow up at a later point in time. That's perfectly acceptable, of course. It should go without saying that you should always follow the prospect's lead on this score; just make sure that both you and the prospect are in agreement as to what the next step will be.

When you come back for subsequent meetings, however, you must bear in mind that unless you have all the information you need with regard to the past, the present, and the future—and unless you have elicited specific suggestions from the prospect on what will be going into your formal proposal—you are still in the interviewing phase. Just as Mark was in the interviewing phase when he showed up for his second meeting, the one the president of the company attended. I usually begin second interviews by saying something along the following lines: "So, Ms. Jones, based on our meeting last time, here are my assumptions . . ." I'll then restate the key points from our last meeting; when I reach a point where new information is required, I'll state my final "assumption" as a framed question, which the prospect is likely to correct.

Words and Phrases for Interviewing

How do you do that?
Who do you work with?
How is that done?
how many
how fast
how often
how much
why
where
who
problems
difficulties
challenges
solutions
answers

procedures
resolutions

In the extended questioning dialogue that follows, we'll assume that the dialogue has been preceded by the essential "small talk," "company biography," and "initial question" steps outlined earlier in this book. By reviewing the next series of questions, you'll see how you can use "how" and "why" follow-ups to establish important information about your target company's past. Notice, too, the way that we use this transitional phrase: "Let me tell you why I ask that." This allows you to briefly cite some of the solutions you've been able to implement with your own customers. (Note that this story is now an excuse to launch into the presentation phase!)

Sample Dialogue

You: So, in the past, **what have you done** when you needed color copies? [Past-oriented variation on Question Number One: What Do You Do?]

Prospect: Let me think. Usually, we just send 'em out to the local copy center. That little place, you probably passed that on the way up. It's called Paul's Copies. They do the color copies for us.

You: Okay. So, if you don't mind my asking, **why have you decided to go that route**? [Past-oriented version on Question Number Four: Why Do You Do It That Way?]

Prospect: Well, it happens so rarely. I mean, I couldn't give you hard figures, but most of the time it's just one or two copies. And it doesn't seem to me that it really happens that often that someone even needs a color copy in the first place. Of course, I don't work in the graphics department, so they may have another take on it.

You: All right. Now, **how much** do you think it's been costing you to make some of those color copies? [Past-oriented variation on Question Number Two: How Do You Do It?]

Prospect: Oh, I have no idea.

You: Just as an estimate, **do you think** seventy-five cents to a dollar would be a good guess? [Past-oriented variation on Question Number Two: How Do You Do It?]

Prospect: Yeah, that sounds right.

You: But as far as you can tell, you don't really use color copies that much? [Past-oriented variation on Question Number One: What Do You Do?]

Prospect: Right.

You: **That's interesting**, because a lot of the people I'm working with are finding that they're relying more and more on the color copying technology that's out there.

Prospect: Well, as I said, this is my perspective. If you'd like, we can go over and meet with Chris, who handles our production work. He may be able to give you a better idea of what we're doing. Maybe we should take a few moments with him before you go.

You: Okay, **that's a good idea**; I may take you up on that. **Let me just check a couple of things** with you here first, though. Let's see. **How many** copiers have you had installed here up to this point? How many machines have you had put in? [Past-oriented version on Question Number Two: How Do You Do It?]

Prospect: We've set up a total of eighteen machines.

You: All right. Now, **how did they all get here?** Were they all purchased at the same time? [Framed, past-oriented variation on Question Number Three: When and Where Do You Do It?]

Prospect: No, no. Each was purchased separately. See, each department had a specific copier that it wanted, specific functions that it was looking for. So we've got probably four or five different brands in the building. To tell you the truth, it's a little bit of a headache when it comes to servicing them.

You: Yeah, I wouldn't be surprised. **Have you had a lot of problems** with breakdowns, paper jams, things like that? [Past-oriented variation on Question Number Two: How Do You Do It?]

Prospect: Well, I imagine it's probably been no more than average, but the real difficulty has come along when someone in, let's say accounting, comes into my office complaining that the copier's down, and I've had to stop and figure out which of the five vendors we're talking about, whether the machine's under a service contract, things like that. If I had to make a guess, I'd say that the actual maintenance necessary has been about average for machines of this kind, but the administrative work that goes into tracking down who's responsible for what has probably been a little above average. Some days it feels like a lot above average, to be honest. That's one of the reasons I'm meeting with you, why I said I thought we should get together when you called the other day.

You: Okay. Now, can I assume that since the machines are all from different vendors, that you haven't taken any steps to connect them and to make them work together on some kind of platform? [Past-oriented variation on Question Number Two: How Do You Do It?]

Prospect: Oh, no. Wow, that sounds like a nightmare, considering all the grief I go through when one of them breaks down . . .

You: Well, **let me tell you why I ask that**. It is actually a lot simpler than I thought it would be at first. **A lot of my clients** are putting together packages that allow them to link the copiers together, which eliminates downtime and means you spend less time talking to a repair person. It also means that when you need to talk to a repair person, everything goes through us so you make just one call.

Prospect: Is that right? You have, what, a universal service contract or something?

You: That's right, we cover everything, handle all the legwork. **You just call us** and we figure out who needs to come down to take a look at the system. So, as I say, that's a feature a lot of my clients have found can win them back an hour or so of telephone time when there's a problem.

Prospect: That's fascinating, because the president of the company is always asking me to try to find a way to spend less time running around dealing with copiers.

You: No kidding. Well, **that's important. It's good to know that that's a priority for you.** All right. Now, in the past, do the departments that make their own decisions about purchasing a new copier **authorize** the purchase orders on their own? [Personalized variation on Question Number Four: Why Do You Do It That Way?] (Note: Group Four questions can address the means by which a person or individual makes decisions and are often phrased indirectly.)

Prospect: No—they go to the president, and he either approves the purchase order or turns it down.

Who's in Charge?

Look what happened near the end of that exchange. It was only at the end that we learned for certain that our prospect is not a formal decision maker with regard to copier purchase. The final question in this sequence was, in essence, a carefully crafted variation of the staring-at-the-notepad gambit for finding out who's involved in the decision-making process. In practice, it would be executed in the same way with our avoiding direct eye contact with the prospect as outlined earlier.

We did learn, however, that our prospect is the person who handles the various crises arising from the five-way maintenance arrangement. So what can we conclude?

Well, we now know that if we want to tear out every copier in the place and replace it with a new one, we're going to have a tough job ahead of us. Not an impossible job, of course, but a pretty tough one. If we want to get our copiers in there instead of the five competing brands that people are currently using, we're going to have to get five department heads to agree to make the change, and we're going to have to line all five of them up in front of the president so he can approve the sale. That's a tall order.

If, on the other hand, we want to implement a system that will allow the company's existing copiers to work more effectively—and, at the same time, allow us the opportunity to take the inside track when it comes to selling the company the next copier it needs when the time comes to expand—then we may be talking to the right person. That's not to say that our prospect is going to make the decision on his own. Odds are he's going to have to make his case in front of the president just like everyone else. But when he does, he's going to be in a position to take advantage of a significant benefit. And that benefit can be seen from any number of angles. That benefit lines up not only with what the company wants (to have our prospect waste as little time as possible on the copiers so he can get back to his other work) but also with what our prospect wants (not to have to spend time trying to figure out which copier is under a service contract, how to get in touch with the appropriate service person, or what to say to the people screaming about breakdowns . . .).

Notice, too, that the feature we thought would be of interest to the prospect—the color copying capability—turned out not to be an important factor. Others in the organization—Chris in graphics, say, or even the president, whom we may end up talking to at some point down the line—may feel differently. But this person, who probably does fit our definition of "someone worth talking to" since he's in a position to move the sale of our linking system along with the president, doesn't think color copiers are of great importance to the organization.

Focusing on the Past

As I said earlier, one of the paradoxes of interviewing is that in order to get to information about the past of a company, you have to talk about the future. But during the interview, after getting past the introduction and small talk, we can start to move to this crucial stage.

Words and Phrases to Ask about a Company's Past
before
previously
in the past

Had you heard about us?
Had you used our services?
Had you used our product?
Did you consider working with us?

Here are some brief exchanges that focus on the target company's past. Each begins with a very important question. At some stage in the interviewing phase, you must work this question into your interview with the prospect!

Example 1

You: Just out of curiosity, **did you ever consider using our company before**? [Past-oriented variation on Question Number Five: Who Are You Doing It With?]

Prospect: No, we never really did. I mean, we'd heard about you guys. We knew you were doing a lot of training with some of the companies in town, but we always assumed that you're out of our league price-wise. I mean, it wasn't a conscious choice never to talk to you; we just never put you on the list because we're under some pretty tight budget constraints here. So when you called the other day, I was a little surprised to hear how you'd worked with some of the firms that face the same kind of cash constraints we do.

Example 2

You: Just out of curiosity, **did you ever consider** working with our packaging firm before? [Past-oriented variation on Question Number Five: Who Are You Doing It With?]

Prospect: No, we hadn't. We'd never even heard of you. That's why I agreed to get together so we could talk. To tell you the truth, I was a little surprised to hear about some of the other publishers you'd been working with. I would have thought that you'd shown up on the radar screen here.

Example 3

You: Just out of curiosity, **have you ever thought about working with our company**? [Past-oriented variation on Question Number Five: Who Are You Doing It With?]

Prospect: You know what? We did. We came awfully close to calling you about a prospecting seminar last year, because I'd heard some really great stories from other people in my industry about the kinds of results you have been able to deliver. Before I could do that, we had some budget problems, and everyone was put on a salary freeze until last February, and I didn't have the training budget anymore. So that kind of put things on hold, then I never really thought about it again after the storm passed.

"You Want Me to Ask the Prospect What?"

During my seminars, when I tell people they need to incorporate this have-you-ever-thought-about-working-with-us question into their interviewing phase, they usually stare at me dumbfounded, as though I just told them that they had to turn in an innocent relative to the police.

They say things like this:

- You mean I have to ask that—straight out?
- You mean I have to ask them whether they thought about working with us—just like that?

- You mean I have to ask the prospect to tell me whether we've ever been on the short list—to her face? Why?

Because maybe you were on the short list once without knowing it! And wouldn't you like to find out if you were? And even if you weren't, posing this question directly—without any double-talk or backing and filling—will tell you a lot about what the movers and shakers in the target company think about your organization. This question may take a little practice to deliver confidently, but I assure you that it's worth the effort.

Asking this question will also give you yet another important indication of how involved your current contact is in the decision making process at the target company.

So take the plunge. Screw your courage to the sticking point and ask the question as I outlined it. Don't sugarcoat it, don't hide it inside another question, and don't apologize for asking. Don't bail out at the last minute and start asking the prospect about his favorite type of music and whether he prefers the Beatles to the Rolling Stones. This is not the time for small talk. Just ask the prospect directly whether he or she has considered using your firm before and follow up appropriately.

PART III

WHAT TO SAY WHEN YOU'RE PRESENTING

All right, now we've moved off the interviewing stage. We've acquired (through artfully constructed framing questions and probing queries) a good deal of information both about the prospect's company and about the prospect as an individual. Now it's time to move ahead to the next stage of the sales cycle.

You've got to present what you're selling.

CHAPTER 10

Active Listening

Before we really roll up our sleeves and start in on presenting, I want to say a few words about listening. Because the art of listening is also an essential part of presentation skills—one that is sadly neglected.

Perhaps the easiest way to distinguish successful salespeople from unsuccessful ones is to watch how they interact with a prospect. Do they do all the talking, never letting the prospect get a word in edgewise? If so, it's a good bet you're looking at a failure.

You must let the prospect speak about him- or herself; the information you'll receive as a result is invaluable. Ramrodding your points through, and merely overpowering the person rather than showing how you can help, is a sure way for you to descend into the stereotypical "hard sell" that no one likes. Such behavior is a great way to lose sales.

To be sure, you and I really believe that our product will help the person we are sitting across the table from. And yet, even though we believe that in our bones, we have to listen, not lecture. Listening is the only way to target the product to the unique set of problems and concerns the prospect presents to us. By staying focused on the objective of helping the prospect (rather than "getting" the prospect), we build trust. And trust is vitally important.

The Salesperson as Helper

When you get right down to it, a good salesperson doesn't so much sell as help. You can pass along important information, and ask for the sale after you've demonstrated clearly how your product can help achieve an important objective; but ultimately, the prospect has to make the decision, not you. Ideally, you have to know what it will take for the prospect to do the selling himself or herself. In this environment, listening becomes very important.

Listening doesn't just mean paying attention to the words that come out of the prospect's mouth. Very little of what we actually communicate is verbal; most is nonverbal. Be sure you're "listening" in such a way that allows you every opportunity to pick up on nonverbal cues. By doing this—letting the prospect get across what's important to him or her—you'll stand out from the vast majority of other salespeople who simply talk too much.

When your prospect wonders something aloud, give the person enough time to complete the thought. When your prospect asks you a pointed question, do your best to answer succinctly, and then listen for the reaction. Allow the speaker to complete sentences—never interrupt. (What's more, you should let the prospect interrupt you at any time to get more information from you.) Express genuine interest in the things the prospect says. Keep an ear out for subtle messages and hints the prospect may be sending you.

When you do talk or make a presentation, don't drone on; keep an eye on your prospect to make sure what you're saying is interesting. If it isn't, change gears and start asking questions about the problems the prospect faces—you are probably missing something important. Of course, you should never come across as hostile or combative to the prospect.

Words and Phrases to Show You're Listening

I see
Really?
Uh-huh

Could you clarify that?
In other words
If I'm understanding you correctly
So what you're saying is
That's interesting
Fascinating

You probably already know that the first ten or fifteen seconds you spend with a prospect have a major impact on the way the rest of the meeting goes. This is because there is an intangible, feeling-oriented, "sizing-up" phenomenon that occurs early on in any new relationship.

Much of who you are and how you are perceived as a communicator—brash or retiring, open or reserved, helpful or manipulative—will be on display in a subtle but crucial manner in the opening moments of your first meeting with someone. Make sure you are sending the messages you want to send. Before the meeting, avoid preoccupations with subjects that have nothing to do with the client; these will carry over even if they never come up in conversation.

The Importance of Note Taking

How do you improve your listening skills? Here's one idea. Always take notes during your meetings with prospects. As we'll see later, this dramatizes your attention and respect for the prospect's needs. (And if you think it's impossible to listen and take notes at the same time, you're wrong; the two actually reinforce each other.)

Once the conversation begins to pick up some steam, take out a legal pad and write down the most important points the prospect makes during your presentation; read essential details back to him or her before the meeting ends. Where appropriate, ask the prospect to expand on key concerns.

That's all very well in theory, you may be thinking. But what if the conversation is going nowhere? How do I listen if there's nothing to listen to? Shouldn't I make a pitch?

Probably not. Early on in the meeting, the odds are that you simply do not know enough about your prospect yet to go into a long presentation. So avoid doing that. Instead, focus your questions on three simple areas: the past, the present, and the future.

What kind of widget service was used in the past? What are the company's present widget needs? What does the prospect anticipate doing with regard to widgets in the future?

Add a "how" and a "why" where appropriate, and that's really all you need. Take notes on the responses you get.

After you reiterate the points the prospect has made, you may be ready to talk in more detail about exactly what you can do to help solve the prospect's problems. But be sure that you listen first.

Active Listening Scenario

Here's what active listening should sound like:

Prospect: What we're mainly concerned with is the turn-around time on our widgets from warehouse to our retail stores.

You: **I see.**

Prospect: At the moment, there's a two-week lag between when a shipment gets to the warehouse and when it actually arrives at stores and can be shelved. That's unacceptable to us. We need something a lot faster.

You: **Uh-huh. I can certainly understand your concern.**

Prospect: A lot of our dissatisfaction with our current vendor stems from their inability to resolve this issue. They say it has to do with the software they use to check the shipments into the warehouse.

You: I see. **So because it takes longer for product to get into the warehouse, that delays its shipment to retail.** Can you give me some more details about the software they're using?

CHAPTER 11

What to Tell
Prospects

I'm willing to bet that more than once—quite possibly several times a day—you've gotten an e-mail where the writer's point is buried somewhere in the fourth or fifth paragraph. Sometimes you probably had to scroll down for what seemed like hours to get to it. Well, I'll tell you a secret: People don't have time to get to the fourth or fifth paragraph. If they read the beginning of a letter and decide it's of no interest, there's a good chance they'll chuck it before they ever get to the point.

It's the same with a speech or a presentation: You have to get to the point quickly. Tell your audience why this presentation should interest them, capture their attention. It's not simple, and it requires a lot of thought.

One of the first things you have to do is to encapsulate what you are trying to accomplish. One of the theories I've heard is that you should be able to summarize your presentation in thirty seconds:

- "I believe that we can provide you with product X at a higher quality and lower cost than you are now paying, and guarantee just-in-time delivery at no extra charge."
- "Our advertising agency has the pulse of the consumers, so we will be able to create believable and effective marketing campaigns for you."
- "I believe our accounting firm can doctor your books much better than your present accountants—and we can even make it seem legal to the IRS."

Okay, maybe that last pitch was just there to see if you're still paying attention. But you get the point. It's only when you've been able to focus on your message that you can begin to sit down and write a presentation.

There are two parts to any presentation. The first part is what you want to tell your prospects. The second part is what they want to hear. A good presentation includes both parts.

Sitting down and writing a presentation can be difficult. However, my experience has shown that when I've successfully done my research, thought about the best twelve people in the company to talk to (a strategy I call the Power of Twelve) . . . well, when I've done that, my mojo is really working and I breeze relatively easily through the most complicated presentation.

On the other hand, when I struggle, when I agonize, it almost invariably means I haven't done my homework. I don't really have a grasp of the situation, and I need to go back and redo parts of the process rather than make a presentation that is doomed to fail.

This is the point at which the words that I'm using are pushed front and center. Sometimes when I'm stuck on a presentation, I make a list of key words and phrases and stick it above my computer screen. Not that I'll necessarily use all of them, but the list is a good reminder of the main points I'm trying to make and the language in which I want to express them.

Use What Works

I know that no matter how much I preach about not doing canned presentations, some parts of any salesperson's pitch will be prepared ahead of time. If you give enough presentations, you start to sense what works and what doesn't. It's perfectly acceptable to use those things that work.

For example, you know your product or service. You know its strengths and weaknesses. Logically, you probably discuss the strengths in every presentation, and you pretty much have that pattern down. The temptation is just to use that. Don't succumb to that temptation.

Remember, the important point isn't how strong your product is. The key point is why that strength is important to your potential customer. How can she use it? Why should she care? The answer to that question is likely to be different for every prospect and therefore every presentation.

Starting Off Right

Another part of your presentation that might be canned is the very beginning. A presentation usually starts with a welcome—a short introduction of yourself and, if applicable, the colleagues accompanying you. Some people go around the room and ask everyone to introduce themselves. It depends on you, your product and service, and the types of companies you sell to. If you're presenting to a single corporate entity, asking them to introduce themselves may be considered frivolous and a waste of time.

Words and Phrases to Begin Your Presentation

Good afternoon
Hello
I want to tell you a little bit about myself
My company does the following things
we make
we do
we create
This is my colleague
I'd like to know who all of you are

Warm-Ups

The important thing in this first part of the presentation is that you insert something that creates a comfort level for you and, if possible, your audience. I saw an interview with Paul Simon once in which he said that he plays the same song first at each of his concerts. I'm not a big Paul Simon fan, but it's the message here that's important.

The tune is apparently an old favorite. The crowd likes it. It warms them up and gets them into Paul Simon. Just as important, both the song and the crowd's reaction to it warm Paul Simon up. This warm-up process gets him into the show.

Everyone should have a warm-up—something that creates a comfort level for you. I still get nervous and I've made probably thousands of presentations of various types over the years. So I imagine you probably do, too.

Here's what works for me. Right after the introduction, I talk about my background and experiences in sales, the number of sales I've made, and the various kinds of companies I've sold to. I illustrate how I have used the sales process that I will be talking about.

This does a couple of things. First of all, it warms me up. It's a part of my presentation that I'm comfortable speaking about. (Some who know me suggest that my comfort level is always high when I speak about myself. But I just ignore them. Where was I? Talking about my comfort level and speaking about myself.)

The other thing it does is let the audience know that I really am an expert, that I do this for a living.

Finally, it paves the way for me to get into the heart of what I want to discuss: the theory behind my sales process, how I developed it, and how I put it into practice.

Words and Phrases for Your Warm-Up

I've been in the business for [x years]
I've been working in [industry] for [x years]
I've worked for [x] companies
experience
background

An associate of mine, a writer who runs a writing training program for corporate executives, always starts his presentation similarly, talking about the fact that he is a writer and brings that expertise to the course. He mentions the newspapers and magazines he writes for and then he holds up his latest book.

He follows that by saying, "Please, I ask everyone to put on your safety belts or at least hold onto your arm rests, because this next thing is really cool."

He then pulls out a Chinese translation of the book he just showed them.

This accomplishes a couple of things all at once. Everyone in the audience chuckles, and probably relaxes a little. My friend relaxes because when that first laugh comes on cue, it means he's on. At the same time, he establishes his bona fides. This isn't a guy who teaches because he can't do anything else. This is a man with impressive real world experience. Most people haven't met any author, let alone one whose works have been translated. And he's done all this with a kind of self-mocking grin so he doesn't come off as a braggart.

CHAPTER 12

The Reason You're There

In the second part of the presentation, after the introduction and your warm-up, you want to explain the topic you are going to discuss and why you think it is valid. As part of this process, you are verifying the information you received and on which you've based your presentation. For example, you might begin this section of the presentation by saying something like this:

"ABC Widgets is the **premier** widget manufacturer in the United States—and has been for **over 150 years**. Your widgets were used on the transcontinental railroad, in the construction of the Brooklyn Bridge, and on every major domestic construction project. But **you are now facing increased competition** from cheaper widget imports that are making inroads domestically. Clearly, you don't want to lose market share. Over **the next half hour** or so, I'm going to tell you a little about **how my company, XYZ Widget Supply Company, can help you**."

Notice that I lay this out in three mini-stages:

1. Here's what the prospect's business looked like in the past (historically important and robust).
2. Here's what the business looks like right now (facing growing competition).
3. Here's what the business can look like in the future (survive and grow with help from my company).

Once you say this (or something like it), you can move on to the next part of your presentation, which is to present the rationale behind your thinking: how buying products from you is actually cheaper for ABC Widgets than buying from its current supplier; how just-in-time delivery can cut ABC's inventory costs; and how all this can be accomplished without any sacrifice in the quality of the finished product.

Then you're ready for part four, which has to do with details: pricing, discounts, the timetable of when you can get started, and any other details you need to fill in. This is a good time to ask for questions. I usually question myself first. How am I going to be able to deliver all this? Can I really guarantee this price? That kind of sets the mood. Often in these presentations, no one likes to be the one to stand up and question anything. But if you're already doing it to yourself, it makes it easier for them.

Finally, the presentation should conclude with a "thank you" and some mention, if not resolution, of what the next step will be.

Words and Phrases for the Second Half of the Presentation

competitive advantage
cost effectiveness
efficiency
cost savings
cost cutting
quality control
customer satisfaction
improve product margins
We can implement these procedures in [x] times
special discount

Take a Look at the View from the Audience

Here are two more basic but important tips. When you sit down to prepare your presentation, you want to write it as though you were going to listen to it. What that means is that you have to put yourself in the mindset of the customer.

I have noticed, for example, that salespeople sometimes gloss over important facts because they seem so obvious to the salesperson who deals with them every day. But what is obvious to you isn't always obvious to your customers. You are always safer assuming that there is someone in your audience who is not familiar with a particular fact.

Another advantage of looking at your presentation from the mindset of your customer is that it allows you to search for missing elements. If you ask yourself what else you would want to know if you were buying from yourself, you'll start to search for holes in your presentation. This lets you plug those holes up before your customers can point them out to you.

Remember the two-part presentation. You know what you want to say. Putting yourself in your customer's mindset forces you to think about what he wants to hear. Think about words that your customer has used in his responses and comments during the interview portion of the sales cycle. These are words and phrases that he uses to describe his business. Find ways of integrating these into your own presentation, since they're more likely to resonate with your audience.

Tell a Story

Finally, as advanced as we are in the realm of communication, with books and television and satellite radio, we are still basically storytellers in the same way we have been since the Stone Age. Grandparents tell their grandchildren about what it was like when their mommy and daddy were young; we regale old friends with anecdotes of previous experiences; we tell stories to our spouses and partners reminding them about how we met and dated.

To the extent that it is possible, it is always better to frame your point in terms of a story. To illustrate, here's a story that a writer friend of mine tells when he makes a presentation to a potential corporate client. I've highlighted those key words that I think make the story more effective.

"When my son was a teenager, I took him in the backyard to build a picnic table. I did it for a couple of reasons. First of all and obviously, there was that whole **father-son bonding thing**. But also, **I grew up in the Bronx**. The most mechanical thing I ever did was to run down to get the building super to come up and fix whatever was broken. A picnic table is a kind of simple project. And I felt building one would **give my son a familiarity with tools that I never had**.

"So we build the table. It's upside down and we're screwing in the last screw. Then we take a nail and carve our names underneath, so that **future generations will know who built this table**. And then we turn it right-side-up and it's just beautiful.

"But there was just one little problem. The only person we could invite to dinner was Shaquille O'Neal, because the table was up to here. [He brings his hand up to his forehead.] And if he came to dinner, he'd have to eat at a slant, because the table was also crooked. [He holds his hand out at a slant.]

"Why do I tell you this story? I had a carpenter come to my house, and based solely on my verbal description of what

I wanted, without benefit of blueprints he did a major expansion of my house. He had the carpentry gene. He was able to visualize and build what I merely described in (believe me) very layman terms. Obviously, I don't have that gene.

"But **if I had taken a basic carpentry course, familiarized myself with the tools of carpentry**, I should have been able to build something as simple as a picnic table. Well, it's the same thing with writing. **Either you have the gene or not.** I cannot teach anyone to write. But **what I can do is familiarize your employees with some of the basic rules of writing** so that they're able to do relatively simple tasks like writing e-mails and memos with greater speed, quality, and confidence."

I really like my friend's approach. What he's done here are a couple of things. First of all, it's a cute story that always gets a laugh. Second, he's created realistic parameters. He isn't promising pie-in-the-sky goals that everyone knows he won't be able to deliver. And he gives assurances that what he can deliver is useful and will profit the company and its employees.

The power of the story is that you visualize it as it's being told. When my friend told me this, I saw him and his son building the table and Shaquille O'Neal sitting there trying to eat dinner at a slant.

His story also raises another important issue. When he started telling it—the story is true, by the way—he identified the person coming to dinner as Kareem Abdul-Jabbar. But as his audiences got younger and younger over the years, fewer and fewer people knew who Abdul-Jabbar was, even though he was one of the greatest centers in the history of the NBA.

I said when you write this you should put yourself in the mindset of your prospects, that when preparing a presentation you want to think about what they want to hear. But you also want to consider your prospects from *the vantage point of their demographics*. If a group is made up of mostly women, perhaps sports references are less apropos than something else. (Please do not send me angry e-mails. I've considered that the previous sentence may not be politically correct. I also know that there are plenty of female sports fans, including many who know more about every game than I do. But we're dealing here with the law of averages.)

Similarly, if you are going to be addressing an older crowd, a reference to rap stars like Jay-Z or Eminem might not be understood. Please do not send even more angry e-mails on this point, as my inbox is already pretty full. I've considered that the previous sentence also may not be politically correct. Plenty of older folks know a lot about rap music. Personally, I know so little that I had to look up the names of those two rappers. The point is this: Know your audience, and figure out what the greatest number of them will likely understand and relate to.

Clearly, a lot of thought has to go into each of your presentations, and the written portion is only one part of what you have to worry about. Here are some lessons to take with you as you go into the meeting room:

1. Get to the point! The best way to write a presentation is to start by summarizing what it is you're trying to say in one sentence. It's a lot easier writing a presentation once you are able to encapsulate your message.
2. Every presentation has two parts: the message you are trying to get across and the message your prospects want to hear. It's important to keep that in mind when writing. Don't just

explain why your product is great; explain why your great product is good for the company you want to sell it to.

3. Don't gloss over facts because you think they're obvious. What is obvious to you may not be to your audience.

4. Be a storyteller. Illustrate your points with stories; for instance, tales of how other companies have used your products.

5. When preparing your presentation, always keep your end game in mind: What is the next step? Do you want feedback, a commitment, or another meeting? That's what your presentation should lead to and conclude with.

This is all good, sound advice. But there's another side to the presentation—a very human side. Like everything else I've discussed in this book so far, it's built on the power of words and how you use them. It's called rapport.

Building Rapport

You are about to enter a large room with a group made up of mostly strangers who hold at least a portion of your future in their hands.

Ideally, you know or at least have met everyone in the room. In the real world, though, you probably don't.

Ideally, you know who is on your side and you know who isn't. In the real world, though, you probably don't.

Ideally, they all know you or at least know about you, and they are in this meeting because they genuinely want to hear what you have to say. In the real world . . . well, I don't have to tell you.

The bottom line: You only have one chance to make a first impression.

I've said repeatedly that sales is a process. But it works on two levels. The first is the obvious one that we've been talking about. You go in for a meeting to introduce yourself and learn about a prospect's company. You know how your prospect can help you—by signing a contract and awarding you the business. But you have to know how you can help her, so you meet with, say, the purchasing manager.

If you work it right, you meet end users, company executives, maybe even the CEO. They provide you with the information you need, and you prepare a presentation that will dazzle them.

One step leads to the next and, while any misstep can derail the entire effort, it's a simple and logical process that makes sense. Sure, you're not going to get the sale every time, but there's generally a reason for it if you don't. You didn't have the right product or service. The price was not right. You couldn't guarantee delivery dates.

But then there's the other level, the one that's subtler. Someone who is important may just not like the cut of your jib. You unintentionally send off bad vibes.

Most of us know that there are a lot of ways people communicate nonverbally. They do it with posture. They do it with their clothing. And each of these things, wittingly or not, tells a little something about ourselves to the people around us.

This is a book about words and using the right words, so I'm not going to spend a lot of time on nonverbal cues you can give during a presentation. Suffice it to say:

1. Dress appropriately. If the company you're presenting to is a button-down sort of place, don't show up in khakis and a polo shirt. Come to think of it, don't do that *anywhere* you present. As a rule, you should dress neatly and professionally. If male, wear a tie and polish your shoes. If female, wear a dress suit.

2. Pay attention to grooming. Visit the bathroom before your meeting, run a comb or brush through your hair, and if you're male, make sure you shaved that morning. For women, simple, unobtrusive make-up and perfume is indicated.

3. Body language is important. Avoid fidgeting, pacing, or repetitive habits such as tapping a pencil. All these things denote nervousness, and that's the last thing you want to convey to your audience.

4. Make eye contact. No one likes talking to someone who won't look you in the eye. That sort of thing makes you look as if you've got something to hide, and we all know you don't. So be confident, prepared, nice looking, and good smelling.

Talk the Talk

Building rapport involves more than just clothing; there are cultural issues, as well. I made a presentation in New York to a foreign-owned company. Everyone there spoke English. But the presentation didn't go well because the people there didn't want to work with me in English. They had their own agenda, and frankly I should have picked up on it well before the presentation. But I didn't. Had I done so, I probably would have prepared handouts in Italian, their language. While I would still have made the presentation in English, that gesture might have been enough to get them to work with me.

That's certainly what happened on a trip to Japan. Perhaps because the culture is so radically different from what I'm used to, I made a special effort to read up about it. I had cards printed up in Japanese as well as some of the handouts. Because I made the effort, my prospects went out of their way to accommodate me.

The bottom line is that because we are becoming much more global in our commerce, it behooves us as salespeople to become more global in our thinking. The country is becoming more diverse, too. I have an Italian contractor remodeling a vacation home I own who has learned Spanish so he can better communicate with his workers.

I'm not suggesting that you go to foreign-language school. But it is important that you learn the customs of your customers. I have a customer who is Indian, and he has a different expectation of the way a meeting should go. Often, decision makers from foreign-owned companies are here on temporary assignment. While many try to blend in and become sensitive to the American way of doing things, quite a few do not. It becomes your responsibility (assuming, of course, that you want to make a sale) to do it the customer's way.

Incidentally, this is not just true for foreign or foreign-owned companies. Although this seems to be becoming less prevalent than it once was, there are (or were) pronounced regional differences in the way meetings are conducted in this country, too. In the South, for example, there's traditionally been more small talk before presentations begin than in the Northeast.

The problem, of course, is that while dressing appropriately or being sensitive to cultural differences probably isn't enough on its own get you the business, not doing so can kill you. Continuing to build rapport during a presentation is the subject of the next chapter. Here are a few things to remember from this one:

1. You only have one chance to make a good first impression.
2. To quote Fernando, the Billy Crystal character from *Saturday Night Live*: "It is better to look good than to feel good." For better or worse, you're often judged on your appearance. The better you dress, the better you will be perceived.
3. Looking good won't win you a sale, but looking slovenly might lose you one.
4. In an age of globalization, it's important that you be aware of cultural and language differences. Behavior that may be acceptable in the United States might be considered scandalous to someone raised elsewhere.

PART IV

WHAT TO SAY WHEN YOU'RE CLOSING

Often, closing a sale seems like the hardest part of the cycle. In fact, I think many times salespeople make it harder than it needs to be. They get intimidated by objections, baffled by obstacles, or—and surprisingly, this is a common one—they forget to ask for the sale. As with everything else in the sales cycle, success in closing is about using the right words to get the result you want.

CHAPTER 13

Overcoming Common Objections

You've wrapped up your presentation with a flourish and sit down in triumph. You can hear the flapping wings of victory, and you're already mentally spending that commission. And then . . . the objection.

This shouldn't come as a surprise. Instead, you should already have anticipated it and have your answer ready. I'm always startled, though, by how many salespeople let basic objections flummox them and throw them off their game.

I really don't like the term "objections." It's better to think of them as responses. When someone tells you there's a problem with what you've proposed, that shows that the person is actually listening and thinking about your products and services. That means you have the opportunity to advance the sale by asking questions, by getting "righted," and by putting the spotlight on your organization's relevant resources.

Responses from the prospect give us the opportunity to gain insight on what the other person is thinking. Calling these responses "objections," on the other hand, sometimes changes the emotional atmosphere for the worse, making it harder for us to ask the right questions. Make no mistake: Asking the right questions is what it's all about at this stage. Somewhere along the line, things went awry. The question is, where?

By raising an issue—rather than flatly rejecting and refusing to discuss your recommendation—your contact is trying to draw your attention to something. Try to ask questions that will help you get to the bottom of whatever it is that the prospect is trying to get you to notice. Remember: Any feedback from the prospect is a form of "getting righted"!

As salespeople, we have to be extremely careful about the assumptions we make when we encounter obstacles late in the sales process. Very often, we hear a negative response and assume that it is an objection, especially when it concerns price. In many cases, the prospect has simply raised an issue that needs to be explored. Sometimes what sounds like an "objection" about your payment terms is really a question about how much flexibility you're willing to show in invoicing. Sometimes what sound like rock-hard **price concerns mask other issues, such as a need to be persuaded about your commitment to follow through**, and a desire to make sure that what you sell actually delivers the benefit you promise.

Let's look at some common objections and the words and phrases that can overcome them.

A few general points first: Here are three simple steps for handling responses effectively:

1. *Identify/isolate* the issues. Ask questions like, **"What makes you say that?"** or **"Why that amount?"** or **"How does this concern fit into your goal of . . . ?"**

   Then ask yourself: **Do I really understand the problems my prospect typically faces? What are these problems, really? (Never forget: Your prospect's initial assessment of an issue may be masking a deeper challenge.)** Exactly how are these particular issues affecting this particular prospect, right now?

2. *Validate* each issue. Figure out what its real-world dimensions are. Talk the challenge through openly and honestly with your prospect. (For instance: **"You're not alone. My experience is that if people have a problem with our delivery dates, it usually comes up at this point in the discussion. Let's see what we can do."**) Don't run away

from the problem or pretend it doesn't exist. Offer appropriate additional information and help your prospect reach a logical conclusion.

3. *Resolve* the issue. This may be easier to do than you think. While every prospect is unique, accomplished salespeople tend to face the same half-dozen or so challenges over and over again within any given target industry. Don't use a cookie-cutter approach, but do share appropriate anecdotes and bring your personal and organizational experience to bear in developing a creative solution.

"I'll Have to Think about It"

If you hear "I'll have to think about it," or some variation on it, after you've made your presentation, say something like this:

You: Well, Mr. Prospect, you know, as I finished this, I have to admit, **I was a little concerned that I might have put too much emphasis on the** (and here pick some nonthreatening aspect of your presentation). **What did you think?**

In a sense, this goes back to the framing technique we explored earlier but in a different context. What you've done here is given the prospect the option to disagree with you. You've deliberately picked a relatively innocuous element of your sales presentation, and you've said to the prospect, "Hey, I made a mistake here, didn't I? Please correct me."

Nine times out of ten, if you've done your preparatory work correctly, and if you say something like the above (expressing your own concern that you may have put too much emphasis on the question of how to train the prospect's people to use your widgets), you'll hear something like this in response:

Prospect: No, actually, it's not the training I'm concerned about. We've just got a problem with your specs. I don't think the people out in Dubuque are going to be able to fit this into their production patterns.

You've uncovered the real obstacle! And from here you can work with the prospect to fine-tune what you have to offer. How do you get around it? Well, I've always been big on "parables." In other words, I believe in telling success stories. As noted earlier, stories are very powerful sales tools. If you can highlight an encounter with a particular customer of yours who did overcome the same or a similar obstacle, do so. If you don't know enough about your customers to be able to do this comfortably, find out!

If you encounter resistance along the lines of "I'll have to think about it" after you've made your formal presentation, isolate a part of the presentation, express your concern to the prospect that you may have mishandled it, and ask for help. In the vast majority of cases, the prospect will reassure you that what you've identified is not in fact the problem, and will say something like, "What we're really still thinking about is . . ."

Words and Phrases to Overcome "I Have to Think about It"

Did you think [x in the presentation] was a little off?
I'm a bit concerned about [x in the presentation].
What do you think?
What's your opinion?
Is [x] a big problem?

As common as "I'll have to think about it" can be, and as frustrating as "I'll have to think about it" can be, it's really not the worst thing that can happen to you at this stage. You want to keep things moving ahead smoothly, and you certainly don't want to run the risk of polarizing the good working relationship you've worked so very hard to develop with your prospect.

Sample "I'll Have to Think about It" Dialogue

You: Well, I think I've covered everything. What do you say? Should we work together?

Prospect: Well, I don't know. I'll have to think about it.

You: I see. I wonder if I could ask you something?

Prospect: Sure.

You: Well, **I'm concerned** that in my presentation I **didn't spend very much time at all** covering the issue of quality control, which I know is of concern to your company. I wonder if **that's something we should discuss further**.

Prospect: No, your presentation points on that were fine. I don't have any worries in that area.

You: Good.

Prospect: But what *does* concern me is the problem of our product launch date. I don't know if you can have your systems revved up in time to meet a very aggressive deadline on this project.

You: I see. Well, **let me tell you about our recent experience** in working with another company that had a very tight deadline . . .

"It Costs Too Much"

I said earlier that many objections should not be taken at face value. This is particularly true of price "objections." Let me give you an example of what I mean. Think about a time you bought an appliance like a stereo or a television. What happened? Perhaps you walked into the store having decided that you wouldn't spend more than, say, $500. Perhaps you gave the store attendant a particular price range when asked about price, and perhaps he or she walked you over to a certain model.

What happened next? You probably found yourself bombarded with reasons why that particular model was just perfect for you. All the person has asked is how much you want to spend, and suddenly you've got this cascade of features coming at you, all apparently based on that one single piece of information: the price. Whatever intelligent interaction there was between you and the salesperson has stopped cold. If you're like me, you're quickly looking for reasons to avoid making a purchase commitment at this point.

Now think about what happens when you run into an intelligent salesperson in a retail setting, someone who's willing to ask you just a few questions about what you're doing, why you're doing it that way, and what you hope to do in the future. This kind of salesperson can often change your "I'm only spending $500" mindset into a "$750 seems worth it" mindset in a matter of minutes, and with very little effort. Haven't you had an experience like that before? I know I have!

The reality is, as salespeople, we often overreact when we hear what we think is a price objection. What we should be doing is getting to the bottom of the issue by asking intelligent questions before we commit to solving any problem the prospect raises.

For example, if the prospect says, "The pricing really isn't what I expected," we must fight the instinct to say, "Stop! Let me tell you why this is a great price!" or "I can *only* cut it by 50 percent!" It might make more sense to explore the issue further by asking, **"What kind of pricing were you expecting?"** Your prospect might respond by saying, "Well, Joe told me he signed on with your company and paid less," or, "Well, I hadn't really thought about it at all." These are two totally different frames of reference! Step back and ask clarifying questions. Use appropriate success stories whenever you can.

Words and Phrases to Overcome "It Costs Too Much"

What did you think it would cost?
How much were you prepared to pay?
What's your ideal price?
What price have you been paying?
What fits within your budget?

Sample Dialogue to Overcome "It Costs Too Much"

Prospect: I'm sorry but your price per widget is out of line with our budget. That's more than I want to pay.

You: I see. I cited $.05 per widget. What were you thinking it would cost?

Prospect: In the past, ABC Corporation charged us $.02 per widget.

You: Interesting. Of course, you indicated that you weren't very happy with the quality of their product, right?

Prospect: Correct. We found that 10 to 20 percent of each lot was defective, which created a huge slowdown in our production line.

You: So your main concern is to keep your production line up to speed, right? To avoid unnecessary delays?

Prospect: Yes, I guess that would be the case.

You: Well, I'll have to talk to my boss, but working with other companies in the industry we've been able to offer a guarantee of a maximum failure rate of 2 percent. If we exceed that rate, we discount on a graduated series of price levels to compensate for lost production hours.

Prospect: That might work for us.

Miscellaneous Objections

Here are a few other common objections:

- Problem: *"We used you a few years ago and had tremendous delivery problems."* There are easy and hard problems. The solution to an easy problem is to only answer the question and avoid reselling. **"I'm sorry to hear that. We have improved our processes since then, and I'm confident this problem won't arise."** For a hard problem, get help from an outside authority who can help you solve the issue.
- Stall: *"Let me run this by my people one more time."* Establish a timetable that works backward from the date of implementation, then articulate the steps that must follow, and determine a necessary decision date. **"That's fine, but I just want to be clear on how much time we've got. The project launches March 3, and we need a signed contract**

in hand by February 3 at the latest. So let's talk again on January 15, which will give us time to iron out any last-minute issues."

- Reassurance: *"With such a young sales force, this could be complicated to implement."* Build credibility. Ask the prospect how he or she was reassured previously about other vendors. Follow that approach, whether it means arranging for a letter of reference, a testimonial, a call to a current customer, or whatever. **"Have you heard about the work we did with KYX Company? I could have someone on their staff write an account of what we provided them and how it worked out. You can also find testimonials to our work on our website."**

- Doubt: *"How many people use this?"* and Fear/Uncertainty: *"Will this really work?"* These responses have to do with a fear of change. The solution is to deal with the transition: Talk about how you will get the prospect started with your products/services and guide them through the initial stages. Take personal responsibility for the success of the program . . . and follow through! **"I understand your concerns, but our service is used by a wide range of people, most recently by the KYX Company with great results. We'll start next month with a trial program and build on that as you become more accustomed to the working arrangement."**

Whatever you do, avoid instinctive "knee-jerk" approaches to problems we assume to be present in the later phases of the sales cycle. Don't be like the telemarketer who called me recently, closed the sale without any negative response whatsoever from me, and then instinctively asked, "Do you need me to bring the cost down a little?"

What If I Get an Outright "No"?

"It's just not right for us."

"I think we'll pass."

"Thanks, but no thanks."

This sort of response is actually quite rare, particularly if you've done your research and followed the advice put forward in this book. You should, though, be prepared for it. The best response to an outright, no-daylight rejection following your proposal is to take responsibility and ask for clarification. After all, if your prospect—after working with you to isolate all the issues and objectives, after telling you everything about his or her objectives in a given area, and after having told you to your face that it was likely that you'd close the sale if you hit all the points the two of you identified together—if, after all that, the prospect can turn around and give you a flat "no," then you've got a right to be surprised. You've got a right to ask where things went wrong.

Remember, though, that the "taking responsibility" **approach is predicated on your well-placed, unshakable confidence in your product or service. Remember that you are not supposed to be angry at the prospect,** but expressing your (no doubt genuine) surprise. And remember that the aim of the technique is *exactly* what you tell the prospect your aim is: to find out where things went wrong so you can work from there!

Words and Phrases to Find Out What Went Wrong

I'm surprised
Can you tell me why?
Can you clarify?
Can you explain?
Could we go over the reasons for your decision?
I'd like you to help me understand

Sample Dialogue about "No"

You: What do you say? Are you ready for us to come together on this deal?

Prospect: I'm sorry. My decision is no. I appreciate your time in presenting to us though.

You: I have to say **I'm surprised at your decision**. I wonder **if you could explain** it to me.

Prospect: My decision is final.

You: I understand that, but **for my own benefit** I'd like to know **what factors might have made you say "yes" instead of "no."** If you could **clarify** what about the presentation or the product doesn't work for you, it would be a big help to me in the future.

Prospect: I can explain, I suppose, but I don't see why it'll make any difference to you.

You: Well, if at some point I present to your company again, **I'd like to know what's important to you** and what are the big factors that influence a decision like this. Also, it would be helpful to me in **making other presentations** to other clients.

Prospect: Okay.

CHAPTER 14

Ask for the Deal

When I get a contract to train salespeople at a large corporation, part of my preparation is to accompany a few of the company's reps on calls. I speak to the sales managers and corporate executives, of course, but it is going "on rounds" with the sales reps that provides me with the best picture of the company, its product, and the way it is sold. As a result, I'm better able to tailor the class to the students' needs.

But one thing I observe regularly—or at least more regularly than I'd like—is a reluctance on the part of salespeople to ask for the sale. Often they'll say something like, "Suppose I call next Tuesday to get your decision." Or "Do you know when you'll make a decision?"

I suspect there are a number of reasons reps don't ask for the sale. Some may be too polite. They feel that asking just then, face-to-face, might put the prospect on the spot, perhaps embarrassing him or her. Or at least I think that's what most of them tell themselves.

But I believe the main culprit is a lack of confidence in their presentations. They don't believe they've earned the sale and want to put off what they assume (usually correctly) will be a "no." If this happens to you a lot (or even a little, quite frankly) there are a couple of points that need to be addressed.

First of all, the bottom line is that you have to ask for the sale no matter how badly you think the presentation went. I can't make it any plainer than that.

Words and Phrases to Use When Asking for the Sale

This program makes sense to me
Your company would benefit

I have a good feeling about this
We could benefit from working together
I'd like to do business with you
How do you feel about it?
What do you think?
benefits
improved profits
results
looking to the future
I feel comfortable

Countering "No"

Why do you have to ask for the sale? For one thing, if the answer you receive is "no," what difference does it make if you find out now or two weeks from now? In fact, finding out that the answer is negative now is probably better for you in the long run; it will keep you from worrying about and dwelling on this sale, and force you to concentrate on another prospect.

I talked earlier about what to do if the prospect says "no." Asking for the sale and getting a negative response has one important advantage: If you get a "no" now, you may be able to find out what went wrong and correct your presentation— before a final decision is made—and salvage the business. I make a special point to ask for the sale if I sense something is amiss. Then, if I'm told I didn't make the cut, I say something like: **"You know, Bill, I was certain I was on track here. Can you tell me where I went wrong?"**

Sometimes I get an answer like, "We just got a new budget and can no longer make as large a commitment to training as we'd anticipated." But often I'll be told a specific area where my proposal went awry. That gives me an opening to try again, to say, **"Gee, I should have thought of that myself. Can I rework this and come back to you with a new proposal?"**

Getting a "no" gives me an opportunity I never would have had if I waited. Waiting typically means getting a response after a decision is made, when it's too late to do anything but turn tail and walk away with as much grace as you can muster.

But there's another issue here apart from how well the presentation went. Not asking for the sale makes you seem less confident in your ability to make the prospect company perform more efficiently, earn more money, and/or put out a better product.

If you lack confidence, you become tentative, making it easy for prospects to say "no" to you. Swagger alone won't necessarily clinch a sale. But a sales rep who demonstrates confidence inspires confidence.

There are a couple of reasons you're not convinced that your product or service is just what the prospect needs. The first is that you haven't done your homework. You haven't spoken to enough people in the company to discover a way to make your product a meaningful part of the prospect company's process. That falls on you. The main focus of the sales product is for you to find a way to make your product seem invaluable to the prospect.

But there's another possible scenario. Perhaps you lack confidence because your product really is inferior to others on the market. That happened to me on one of my earliest jobs. I was a good, aggressive salesman, and at first I was able to make a decent enough living, at least for a single young man—even one who lived in Manhattan. But it got to me after a while.

Often the sales I made were because my company was willing to cut prices to the bone, not because the product was the best choice available. Proof of that is that there were very few repeat orders.

I quit after only about six months, determined never to put myself in that kind of situation again. I was young, carefree, and a little idealistic. I know we don't all have those choices, but this is something we should strive for.

CHAPTER 15

Follow Up with a Flourish

You've given your presentation and, in an ideal situation, the stars are aligned. Everyone agrees that what you're selling is not only perfect for the company but you can deliver it where and when it's needed in just the right form that it's needed. Moreover, the price you charge not only allows you a nice profit but it is much cheaper than the company can get for similar (and inferior) products anywhere else.

And then you wake up.

Surely, some dreams come true. But more often than not the end of the presentation does not coincide with the end of your work on the account. I typically end my presentations by summarizing the main points I've already made:

We'd like to work with you

Here's why we'd like to work with you

Here's why we think we are the right company for you

We share your vision. We understand what you are trying to accomplish

If this is one of those dream-come-true moments (see earlier), you'll close the deal right then and there. Or someone will tell you, "Give me a call Tuesday and we'll finish this off."

However, usually the onus stays with you. You will have to follow up. Most salespeople say, "I'll call you in a week to get your reaction."

I don't believe in that. Unless I'm specifically told otherwise ("I'm going to be out of town. Check back with me in two weeks"), I always call back two to three days after a presentation so that it is still fresh in their minds. And I never start that conversation by saying "Do you have any questions?" or "Have you any thoughts about us?"

Your prospect is never prepared for your call or ready to ask you questions.

Instead, you should start the conversation by saying something like this: **"I'd like to put together a work order"** or **"I'd like to block out dates for my seminars with you."**

No matter what you sell, it's important that you know the company's ordering cycle. Does it place orders weekly, quarterly, or annually? Are supplies replenished on a continuing basis under terms of a contract that runs out next week, next month, next year? If you sell corporate insurance, are the company's existing policies coming up for renewal?

Knowing this cycle offers several advantages. First of all, it shows you are on top of the situation, that you've put some thought into the process, and that you know what's important. It makes you look good.

Second, when you do make the follow-up call, it's an easy way to get a meaningful conversation going: **"I know the policy/contract/current buy cycle (pick one) is about up, so it might be a good time to start thinking about how to word a purchase order."**

Words and Phrases for Your Follow-Up

I'd like to

I thought I'd send you

This might be a good time to

Let's set a date

Let's agree to another meeting

Let's start this project together

Finally, knowing the purchase cycle will let you know when it's time to start beating a dead horse. At a meeting in January, a potential client assured me he wanted me to address his national sales meeting in May. When I hadn't heard anything further from him by the beginning of March, I placed a call to him. A couple of weeks later, I placed another.

You'd think that a guy who is in charge of sales would have a little sympathy for a fellow salesperson and at the very least return a call. He didn't, but that happens, too. We've all met the guy (and excuse me, my experience is that it's always a guy) who is so wrapped up in himself he never returns calls.

Based on my couple of meetings with him, I didn't peg him to be like that. So I placed a couple more calls, none of which were returned. Perhaps he was busy. Perhaps he really wanted to use me and was tied up. Perhaps I was delusional.

I knew that arrangements for his meeting would have to be finalized at least six to eight weeks in advance. When I didn't hear from him by early April, I knew it just wasn't going to happen. I'd missed that buy cycle and I had to move on. Sometimes you just have to punt.

Has the Fat Lady Sung Yet?

Most important, knowing the buy cycle is a good way to remind yourself that sometimes it ain't over, even though the fat lady sang.

A woman I know in Atlanta—let's say she sells widgets—gave what she thought was a brilliant presentation. When she left the conference room, she was certain she'd clinched a sale. But she was wrong. Somehow she'd misread one of the company's needs as well as the level of dissatisfaction with its existing widget supplier. Now let us move forward ten months. It is time for the company to reorder widgets. This woman refused to believe it was all over. She claimed she never heard the fat lady sing.

She wanted to go back in and make another presentation, a better presentation, but didn't know how to do it. The question is: How do you start another conversation when much of what you plan to say is exactly the same as the last conversation you had?

The salesperson came to me and described the situation. I advised her to admit that she made a mistake, to go back to her contact and be frank about it: **"We missed the boat and we'd like another shot."**

The salesperson was shocked. "I've been taught that you never apologize, never admit defeat, and never say you did anything wrong."

When I asked her why, she was stumped. So she tried my idea, and her contact told her not to worry. Her original presentation wasn't off by as much as she thought, and she'd made some very good points. Moreover, the prospect told her where her first presentation had gone astray—all items were easily correctible. Of course she could come back. And she did.

Because she knew the sales cycle, she knew when to hit the prospect again.

There are several lessons to take away from this chapter: Chief among them, don't wait a week or longer to follow up on a presentation. Call your contacts within a few days, when the presentation is still fresh in their minds. Don't ask if they have any questions; ask for the sale. Use words and phrases that show you're ready and willing to move forward.

Knowing the sales cycle for your product or service is helpful in many ways—most notably in terms of when the timing is best to ask for a contract. The more you can show by your word choice that you understand the deadlines your prospect is on, the more easily you'll turn him or her into a client.

Sometimes, if a prospect says one thing and does another, you may have to punt. Time is one of your assets. You don't want to waste it where someone clearly isn't interested. Not every sales call will result in a sale. If it did, we'd all be a lot richer. At the same time, if you made a mistake, don't be afraid to admit it. It's one way to restart a conversation and ignore any singing you may have heard in the background. Sometimes it ain't over even when the fat lady has exited stage left to tumultuous applause.

Conclusion

We've looked at a lot of different words and phrases, and how using them creatively can take you through the sales cycle and end in happiness: You get the sale, the client (no longer a prospect but a *client*) gets what she or he wants, and everyone wins. As I've stressed, words are your tools in this process; but like any tools, you have to use them correctly to get the results you want.

Here, in simplified form, are my basic rules for sales success. Obviously, sometimes you'll run into a complex situation that requires some fancy footwork. But nine times out of ten, if you follow these rules and choose your words and phrases based on them, you'll do just fine.

- Don't underestimate the importance of prospecting.
- Monitor your prospecting results. What are your ratios?
- Ask key people what they're trying to accomplish in the area in question. (When you do, you will automatically distinguish yourself from your competition.)
- If you're finding that, over and over again, you're losing sales because of the same objection—say, that your price is too high—you are probably facing some problem on an organizational level. Take the time to talk to your sales manager about your company's strategies and market position.

- Once you have made contact by telephone, build your first in-person visit upon your past discussion with that contact. Don't begin from scratch as though you'd never spoken with your contact before! If possible and appropriate, mention some memorable element or remark from the earlier phone conversation. This will move the prospect away from the "it's-time-to-talk-to-some-salesperson" mindset and toward the "this-is-that-interesting-person-from-that-interesting-company" mindset.
- Don't obsess on a single account. I worked with one woman who boasted that she had visited a single account thirty-three times before closing. That may sound impressive, but what if the time she spent on that call could have been devoted to prospecting efforts that would have led to two (or, quite possibly, considerably more) sales?
- Don't try to present during the interview stage.
- Don't confuse a presentation with a demonstration. The presentation is what you do after you've gotten all the information you need from the prospect during your interviewing stage. A demonstration of your product or service may take place much earlier; it's something you do to elicit interest at an earlier point in the sales cycle.
- Visit the prospect's manufacturing facility or other "real-world" environment.
- Encourage the prospect to visit your office.
- If your selling environment and industry are appropriate for it, consider using visual aids.
- Don't place too much emphasis on reams of reports, color brochures, or elaborate pie charts and regression analyses. Deluging the prospect with information is a common and

costly mistake. As a general rule, prospects will have a hard time forming a positive view of anyone or anything when forced into information overload; salespeople usually ignore this and pile the paper on anyway.

- When you take notes, take notes! Don't take notes so the prospect will think you're taking notes. Take notes! (I once met with a telephone system salesperson who asked whether I'd mind if he took notes during our meeting. Of course, I said I had no problem. He pulled out a single crumpled piece of paper and a ragged, chewed-on ballpoint pen. As I told him what we were looking for in our next system, he smiled and nodded, and over the course of the next half hour wrote down one thing on that piece of paper. He wrote the number eight. That was how many lines there were in our office. What kind of proposal do you think he was able to put together based on notes like that?)

- Bear in mind that by introducing price during the interviewing stage you are relieving much of the pressure from the prospect. (For many prospects, you will probably be passing along the extremely valuable information that your service costs less than they think.)

- Don't place too much trust in media accounts about the objectives of your target company. The media are often wrong. Reading articles or watching television programs may be an important adjunct to your interviewing and verification efforts, but it can't replace them.

- Remember that you're working with an individual (or with a group of individuals), not an institution. You represent your company, yes; but your company isn't making the presentation, you are. Establish a relationship between two people, not two corporate entities. Tell your prospect that you want the business, not that your company does.

- Find out how decisions relating to purchasing your product or service have been made, or how decisions relating to similar purchases have been made. Odds are that the decision about your product or service will be made in essentially the same way. Specifically, if you learn that the decision has always been made by a committee in the past, find a way to make your presentation directly to that committee. Don't waste your time with a single member of the committee if you can possibly avoid it.

- If you and your prospect face a considerable gap in age or in some other aspect of your professional demeanor—if, for instance, you are a woman in your mid-twenties trying to close a dyed-in-the-wool "good old boy" in his mid-sixties who can't seem to bring himself to treat you as a professional equal—consider making your presentation with another member of your organization, someone who may be able to put your prospect at ease. (This "escalation" technique is also particularly effective when you're dealing with a prospect who needs reassurance that he or she is making the right decision.)

- Aim high; don't assume you can't make your presentation to the top person in an organization. Even if this person does not make the final decision regarding the product or service you have to offer, he or she can be a powerful ally. Try starting at the top, eliciting "power referrals" from the top people in your target organization.

- Be ready for common objections and don't be caught off-guard by obstacles that are typical in your field. (If you think back, you'll probably recall that this has happened to you on a number of occasions. Many sales are lost when salespeople are surprised by prospect queries and comments that should really come as no surprise at all.)

- Keep your promises. People will remember you.

APPENDIX

Sample Sales Dialogues

Here's a complete sales scenario, from start to finish, complete with requisite small talk and resistance from the prospect. I've highlighted key words and phrases to show you how they easily and naturally slot into conversations such as these. Think of what follows as a model for developing a good conversation. That's what makes effective selling possible.

FIRST APPOINTMENT

You: Hello, how are you?

Prospect: Fine.

You: **Good to meet you.**

Prospect: Nice to meet you, too.

You: I had an interesting time getting over here because of the traffic; do you guys have a lot of traffic around here?

Prospect: Always—they are doing major construction this year on Main Street. There is a lot of traffic.

You: Really? Now, do you live far from here?

Prospect: I live about an hour away, and these days it's about an hour and a half with the traffic—it's really trouble. Do you want to sit down?

You: Thanks. I walked through the building—**you have an interesting facility. What do you actually do?** You manufacture chairs?

Prospect: Yes, we manufacture chairs, and office furniture. We design and produce all kinds of furniture: everything for an office top to bottom, and for upper-scale organizations and executive offices, too.

You: No kidding. **How long have you been in the business?**

Prospect: We've been in business for twenty-five years.

You: Really?

Prospect: And we've grown from a mom-and-pop business at the beginning to the point now where we are ready to bring the company public in a few months.

You: No kidding, that's fantastic! Okay. Do you remember our telephone conversation at all?

Prospect: Not really.

You: Let me ask you a question. **Would it help if I tell you something about me and my company first?**

Prospect: Yeah, that would definitely be helpful.

You: Let me give you a little background. We've been in business for the last twenty-two years, and **we've worked with about a thousand different companies** selling our widgets. One of the things we've found is that our widgets have been extremely **beneficial** in a number of areas. I'm just curious though, in the past **have you ever bought widgets from an outside vendor?**

Prospect: We tend to do everything on the inside whenever we can.

You: That's unusual. Why is that?

Prospect: To save money; we believe that it saves us money.

You: Uh huh.

Prospect: And it's just one of those things; that's just the way we've done it for years.

You: No kidding, and you still manufacture X, Y, and Z? **How many widgets are you using today?**

Prospect: Hmm, I have to think.

You: The reason I'm asking is, I've been working with a number of companies, and, you know, **it's something that they found needed to be revisited** based upon current demand.

Prospect: We've been really backed up—we have a lot of orders for some reason for the upcoming year. We've been so bombarded that we haven't taken the time to analyze it. We've increased from our normal widget use, which is about 25 a day, and we've gone up to 75 to 100.

You: Have you really?

Prospect: Yeah, but we just haven't had time to think about it.

You: That's incredible. **That seems like a lot of work.**

Prospect: Yeah, it has been. We just got the report last week when we realized that we had to place more material orders.

You: You know, when I was driving up, I realized there seem to be more trucks around your building than there were a year ago. **It seems to me that you're growing.**

Prospect: Yes, like I mentioned, this year has been crazy. We haven't had a chance to sit down. We're going public and we're growing. It's just hectic.

You: I'm just curious how, you know—you look like you actually like this kind of job. I mean, it seems like an exciting company. **How did you get this job? Why do you stay here?**

Prospect: Well, first of all I love the business. Actually, my grandfather started the business and left it ten years ago.

You: Really.

Prospect: Then, it went out of the family. Other people were managing it and running it, and then I came back into it after I got my MBA. I just love this company so much.

You: How long have you been back?

Prospect: I've been back for six years.

You: **Is it working out the way you expected it to?**

Prospect: Better! This going public thing is my baby, and I'm enjoying it.

You: And the decision to produce your own widgets—that really came from some years back?

Prospect: Yeah. It's been like that for many years, and like I said before, we've never had the time to think about it, it's always been so hectic.

You: You never thought about doing that outside?

Prospect: No. The fact is, you know, when you called, that's probably why I made the appointment; it was probably a thought to go outside.

You: I'll tell you what my thinking is and the reason why I'm asking you all this. We have been working with other manufacturers, and what we are finding is that **the widgets we produce really have been able to save them time and money**. But more importantly, they actually **enhance the overall productivity and the value of the end product** being sold.

But let me go back to one thing: In the past you typically manufactured from here, but if you would change, **would that drastically impact the people who are working here**? I don't want to do something to throw somebody off.

Prospect: Well, it could, it could. There are three people who are involved in taking the material and creating the widget, which then goes into the rest of the machinery. But the truth is, I wanted to promote them and get other people to do this, because it is kind of grunt work.

You: Having worked with a lot of manufacturers before, I think that **there are a host of things that we can produce to help you**.

Prospect: Well, yes. But can I tell you something really honestly? The only hesitation I have, even with just talking to you, is the quality. We know when we make it inside that we are not going to have any problems in that area; and, of course, we never did it on the outside. Other companies in the industry have had problems, as you know, with their widgets, so quality is an issue. Actually, doing it inside wasn't really that big a deal.

You: Would you mind if I showed you one of our widgets? Let me just show you this—take a look at this. I think the thing that I like best when you look at widgets, one of things that this widget does, which **probably no other widget does**, is that it has this little hinge here. See that? That's patented. That's an input-output control flow through valve. That's what keeps our **quality standard** the highest in the industry.

Now, if I were thinking about making widgets for you, I would try to make a widget that featured that hinge.

Prospect: The only thing is, when I look at that picture, I don't know what size that is, but we tend to need it larger.

You: Uh huh . . . larger . . .

Prospect: Because of our machines. I'll tell you our situation. We have some rebuilds, which are the old machine version, and we have some new machines. That's why we need primarily larger widgets than the size you have. And I think some might have to be customized.

You: How much larger are you talking about?

Prospect: Probably 3 to 6 inches bigger than that.

You: Take a look at this—if we did it this way would that work?

Prospect: How about a little smaller?

You: A little smaller, okay . . . Say, I'll tell you what. Let's change the configurations, and come back with a 350 over 90, like this model. And if we did this configuration **I think this would do what you wanted**.

Prospect: Right. Because then I could use it for the older machinery and the newer machinery.

You: You know what? It might help. Let me tell you something. **I think it might help if you and I went into the plant**

now; that way I could **see how this whole thing operates**, and what it looks like, and how your people are actually using what we're talking about.

Prospect: Yeah, if you are going to customize it, I would love for you to come with me now, and really look at everything and make sure it's right.

You: Okay, let's do that.

• • •

You: It was really interesting what you showed me, what I found out about **how you actually do business**.

Prospect: Oh, yeah. I mean people think that we're this little specialty place, but when you go down on the floor it's just another world.

You: Yeah, it really is interesting what you do. I have an idea, and you tell me how you think this works. I could come back with a proposal, because I think that you could use about 500 of the widgets at any given time. What I would like to do is come back some time in the next ten days, probably next week, if that's all right with you.

Prospect: Wait, let me check my calendar.

You: But let me tell you what I'll do. **Let me come back and bring you** not a proposal but an outline. What I like to do is sit down with Jill, Andy, and maybe I'll get Steve involved in this, and actually **develop an outline of how I think this would work**. That way we'll be one step before the proposal still.

Prospect: I'll get my production manager in on this.

You: Would you?

Prospect: Yeah.

You: Why don't we do this. **Let's get together next Thursday.** Let me come back with an outline. Let me also put together some prices.

Prospect: Okay, that would be very helpful.

You: By the way, just out of curiosity, typically when you look at your **pricing structure** now, how would you say it's running?

Prospect: It's been between ten and twenty per gross, depending on quantity.

You: Is it really? Okay, let me play with that. Okay, let me come back, let me work from this, and let's talk next week, if you don't mind. **I might call you beforehand** just to run a couple of things by you.

Prospect: Oh, yeah, that will be fine.

You: Okay, let's get together Thursday, let me show you what my thinking is, and we'll see if we can go from there.

Prospect: Okay, that sounds great . . . Can we make it for 11:00 on Thursday?

You: That would be great. And what I might do is bring Lynne with me. I'm not sure, but we'll talk about that later.

Prospect: Okay, does Lynne know this stuff?

You: Lynne is great. I'll tell you one of the reasons why I'm saying that. Lynne has **had experience in this area before** and she might have a different take on this . . . but in any case, I'll review this with her. Let's play it out, and let me come next week and we'll go from there.

Prospect: Okay.

You: Great, thanks a lot.

Prospect: Thank you.

SECOND APPOINTMENT

You: Good to see you again.

Prospect: Hi.

You: How are you.

Prospect: Our production manager couldn't join us—we had a little incident on the floor.

You: Uh oh.

Prospect: But he really did give me some information, and we discussed the issues, and now we are really eager to see what you have come up with.

You: **All right. Okay, let me tell you what I did.** Let me tell you what happened. I went back to the office and met with Steve, Lynne, and Jill.

Prospect: Was Lynne going to meet with us?

You: She had to take a rain check. Next time, maybe she will be able to get together with us. In any case, what happened was I talked to her and what we came up with was this. I didn't do a proposal, what I did was a **preproposal**, an outline, as we discussed, and basically **what I did was structure**. I set out on what I thought **your objective** was, how I thought we might work together, what I thought the cost would be, what I think the **savings** might be to you ultimately, and a shot at a **production schedule**. That's how I put this together. And I would like to run this by you, and if you like it we can go ahead.

Okay, anyway, let me go through this with you if that's okay. Here's my copy, here's yours. All right, now, let me show you how it happens. Based on the problem that we talked about, first of all, this is what I think our objectives are, what I think you want to do, at least what I understand about your objective, but it's possible you might want to change it.

Prospect: Right.

You: Okay, **so you agree with what we have laid out here**?

Prospect: Yeah. I think you've hit it on the head.

You: Now, the second thing was to **analyze the situation**. We went in there, we looked at it, we talked, and we looked at the model TJ38 as a possibility. We felt that this was the kind of program that would work for you. So, this is what it is. So, I figure that now what we want to suggest is the program where you are using is on a level here, which will produce this kind of **result**. And that's a range I think would make sense.

Prospect: Um, not really. I mean it does but it doesn't.

You: **Tell me what you think.**

Prospect: Well, in terms of quantity on the initial shipment.

You: **Uh huh.**

Prospect: You know, you base that directly on what we are using now, and we're going public; we have a small storage area.

You: Uh huh.

Prospect: We could increase that at the end. But at first that might be kind of high.

You: Okay.

Prospect: Yeah.

You: Okay, let's cross this off. Now **I'm a little worried** about this part. **Do you like this element here**, element three, that says the minimum will be 14,000?

Prospect: Yes, that I liked.

You: Okay, but this you don't like.

Prospect: No . . . just because it wouldn't be enough, I need a good sampling to start it, not large quantities.

You: Okay, what about item number four, does that make sense to you?

Prospect: Um, not really, no.

You: No . . . Okay, let's take that out. Let's take out items three and four.

Prospect: Uh huh.

You: Here's a plan we've used with some of our customers. Take a look at this. (Pause.) Now this is what I would say. I would rather see you do it this way. What do you think about that?

Prospect: Ah, that's better.

You: **Do you think that makes sense?**

Prospect: Uh huh.

You: Let's get rid of three and four, and let me add this item.

Prospect: Uh huh.

You: Does that make sense?

Prospect: Yeah, now that little thing . . . is that the test drum?

You: Yes.

Prospect: Could we do that . . . How soon could you do that if I'd agree?

You: Well, I could **speed up the process**, I had thought about this timetable over here, and here was my conclusion at the time. I thought this would work okay. I thought that Tom could do about ninety and if you want to, he could do about eighty . . . even sixty if you wanted that.

Prospect: I think eighty would be fine.

You: Okay, that works with an eighty-day max. Now that we move down to here, here's the cost . . . my estimation is **it will cost you about this much**. So that's how I see the cost coming out. Here's my point—and I will show you the other piece of this outline—my point is, based on this cost, this will save you about three cents per unit, which you will multiply by 150,000. You start to see what happens. That's why my question on this part over here . . . now at first I wasn't happy with that number.

Prospect: Yeah, that is a bit high.

You: Okay, **I wasn't happy with that. I thought we could do better.** When I went back to John, he thought if you commit to this minimum purchase, I could change that number, which would reduce the cost to about here.

Prospect: Let me ask you something.

You: Yeah.

Prospect: Um . . . once we go public in a few months, we'll have the cash.

You: Right.

Prospect: But right now that's a lot of money for us . . . doing it ourselves, you know, the cost is kind of spread out.

You: Right. Uh huh.

Prospect: Could we do that for the test? Do the test run for the lower, at the lower price, and make up for it later?

You: That's an issue. **Suppose I billed it out, not immediately**, suppose I give you sixty days on the billing process. Zero up front, you stay with this piece that we talked about, but I give you sixty days **without any kind of payment**, and then, assuming everything is all right, we will drop the whole payment in at that point. **Is that better for your cash flow?**

Prospect: Yeah, actually that would work out very well.

You: All right.

Prospect: We can get the bank's signature, if you need to.

You: Now, I know your brother is involved in production. Did you talk to him at all about this?

Prospect: Yeah, Bill wanted to see the pricing.

You: That would be no problem.

Prospect: And make sure it's in his budget. He said it would probably get rid of the grunt work.

You: Yeah, okay. Let me ask you a question, should we go to Bill?

Prospect: No, it's not necessary.

You: If I come back with a proposal and I write this up, will Bill have any problems, or do you think that's a concern?

Prospect: Um, I don't think so. Bill is very . . . Since I've come on, he has always helped me with anything. When I brought this up, he said "Great" . . . and to be honest with you, actually, I would make that decision. As it turns out, my brother is not going to be involved in this company much longer.

You: Really.

Prospect: He wants to go outside and do some consulting on his own. We believe it will work out for the best for everyone.

You: Okay. So let's do this. Let me take what we have just done now and, if you agree with this, we will look at these basic components. Let me **put this together in a full proposal**, let me come back in . . . give me a week or so, because I have to get it all set up on the computer.

Prospect: Okay.

You: And then what I want to do is begin to think about how we would put this together. I'll tell you what I'm going to do, if you don't mind. I would like to start to reserve this inventory. Now I know you don't need it for another ninety days, so what I'd like to do is hold that initial quantity in abeyance, so we have it. That way it's not a problem meeting your schedule.

Prospect: Um, I'm not so sure about that.

You: Why? Tell me.

Prospect: Just because I have to see the proposal, see everything before I just commit to that.

You: Well, okay.

Prospect: With the real pricing.

You: Okay, so the **cost might be a concern**. Let's go back to this. If that's a concern then what . . . I guess what I'm asking you is, **what would make this work better**?

Prospect: Well, you analyzed the cost.

You: Right.

Prospect: On how much we would save, and the savings aren't that great.

You: Okay.

Prospect: It's good, but it's not a lot. I have gotten some literature from your competitors and . . .

You: Have you talked to the Johnsons?

Prospect: I didn't talk to them, I talked to the Petersons.

You: Oh really. Oh.

Prospect: They didn't send a salesperson or anything like that, but they did send me literature.

You: I have to tell you something—they have very good prices. I can't argue with that.

Prospect: And I have to consider that. And quality, too, of course.

You: Okay.

Prospect: What I would love to do is speak to some of your customers.

You: I'll tell you what I would do. **I have my references here.** Let me give you the list. Call them, and I think you'll like what you hear. I have to be honest—**I see this as making a lot of sense for your organization**.

Prospect: Uh huh. Um, well, maybe I just really want to see the proposal.

You: Okay. That's fair.

Prospect: That would make me feel better.

You: Okay, then let's get together.

Prospect: Okay.

You: Okay, let's do this: Do you have your calendar? Let's get together on the eighth.

Prospect: Okay.

You: Let me come back, and let me put a whole proposal together. I am still going to block out this inventory at our risk and I will tell you why: because if I get you to say you want to do this, I would like to have the inventory for you.

Prospect: Okay, that's fair. I don't want to make you go out on a limb, though . . .

You: No, no. I just want to make sure you're okay if it goes through, that's all. And that's our risk.

Prospect: Okay.

You: Okay. I'll see you on the eighth. Let me bring back the proposal and we'll discuss it. Look, if you think Bill should be here, we can always have him come in, if that's not a hassle, but we'll work that out.

Prospect: Yeah. Bill could drop by.

You: Okay, good. See you next week.

Prospect: Okay.

You: Thanks a lot.

THIRD APPOINTMENT

You: How are you?

Prospect: Good.

You: That's great. **I gotta tell you something. I was very happy with our last meeting.** I thought it went well and I like everything that we did.

Prospect: Yeah. I mean the truth is that I've never been with a salesperson that showed me such detailed attention and came back again.

You: I appreciate that.

Prospect: They mostly come in and give pricing and leave. That's it.

You: You know what's helpful. **It's helpful for me to understand what you do, and the way you do it, and how you do it, and where you do it, and who you do it with.** So finding out about all that really gave me some information. Let me tell you what I have in my briefcase. In my briefcase I have a proposal for you that I think is right. I went ahead and I changed a couple of the minor things I talked about that I wanted to make right, and basically I think you're going to like what I have. **I feel very comfortable with it.**

Prospect: Good.

You: Let me show you. Here it is. On the first page is a letter saying we want to do business with you. I just want you to know that whatever else we do, I would love to do business with you. This simply says what we pretty much outlined. Here is a little about us, who we are and what we do. Okay, here is the product we've designed for you, TJ38 minus 3, and here we're saying this is the quantity. This is what it's going to look like.

Prospect: Do you have that sixty-day thing?

You: Yes, that's right here.

Prospect: Yeah, okay. Let's get started.

You: Thank you very much.

Prospect: Okay. Thank you.

Index

Abdul-Jabbar, Kareem, 162
Appointments
    getting, 12–18
    sample dialogue for, 202–17
    setting, 18–19
Attention, getting, 13–14
Audience mindset, 160–64

Body language, 166
Buying cycle, knowing, 191–92

Charts, 78, 115, 196–97
Closing deals
    asking for deal, 183–87
    follow-up during, 189–94
    importance of, 8
    overcoming objections during,
        171–82, 198–99
    strategies for, 183–87
    words for, 184–85
*Cold Calling Techniques (That Really
    Work!)*, 19
Cold calls
    appointment setting, 18–19
    identifying self, 14–16
    introducing self, 13–14
    mechanics of, 12–19
    questioning statements for, 17–18
    reasons for, 15–17
    responses to, 57–70
    sample cold call, 20–21
    script for, 19–20
    strategies for, 11–21
    successful cold call, 20–21
    voicemail messages for, 35–38
"Costs too much" objection, 177–79

Crystal, Billy, 168
Cultural issues, 166–68
Customer mindset, 160–64

Deal, closing
    follow-up during, 189–94
    strategies for, 183–87
    words for, 184–85
Decision-makers
    as allies, 198
    being in charge, 138–39
    building rapport with, 74, 119
    new decision-makers, 123–24
    reaching, 106, 110–15, 118,
        138–39
Demographics of audience, 160–64
Demonstrations, 196
Dress tips, 166, 168

E-mails
    composing, 41–56
    length of, 42
    message text for, 47–51
    P.S. for, 53–54
    restating message in, 54–55
    samples of, 48–50, 55–56
    signature for, 51–53
    strategies for, 42–44
    style of, 42–44
    subject line for, 44–47
*E-mail Selling Techniques (That Really
    Work!)*, 42
Eminem, 163
Escalation technique, 198
Eye contact, 113–14, 131, 138, 166

Feedback, 164, 172–73. *See also*
   Responses
Follow-up
   for phone conversation, 28, 38–39
   tips for, 189–94
   words for, 28, 191
Framing questions
   essential questions, 82–92, 112–13
   general questions, 98–99
   leading questions, 99–101
   power of, 93–104
   responses to, 102–4
   sample of, 104
   six-question model, 82–92, 112–13
   specific questions, 99
   words for, 97

Globalization concerns, 166–68
Grooming tips, 166

"Hard sell," 79, 146

Identifying self, 14–15
Interview
   essential questions for, 82–92,
      112–13
   first phase of, 73–79
   framing questions for, 82–104
   importance of, 8
   note-taking during, 76, 104
   presentations and, 196
   price and, 159, 197
   questions for, 74–77, 81–92
   sample scenarios for, 90–92
   six-question model for, 82–92

talking too soon, 75–79
   words for, 13–14, 71–74, 79,
      133–34
Introducing self, 13–14
Issues and objections
   isolating issues, 173
   overcoming, 171–72, 198–99
   resolving issues, 174–78, 195, 198–99
   validating issues, 173–74
   words for, 175, 178, 182

Jay-Z, 163

"Last resort" query, 112–15
"Lemons into lemonade," 59–61
Listening
   art of, 145–50
   examples of, 149–50
   importance of, 66
   improving skills, 146–49
   note taking and, 148–49
   to presentations, 160–61
   prospecting and, 145–50
   words for, 147–48

Media concerns, 197
Messages for voicemail
   for cold calls, 35–38
   effective messages, 23–39
   examples of, 25–26, 28–31
   follow-up for, 28, 38–39
   sample voicemail, 38–39
   for team calling, 31–33
   telephone tag and, 33–35, 37–38
   words for, 26

"Need-based" selling, 89
"No" responses, 58–66, 181–82, 185–
   87. *See also* Responses
Note-taking
   importance of, 148–49
   during interview phase, 76, 104
   for proposals, 197

Objections
   isolating issues, 173
   overcoming, 171–82, 198–99
   resolving issues, 174–78, 195,
      198–99
   sample objections, 69–70, 176,
      178–79, 182
   validating issues, 173–74
   words for, 175, 178, 182
Obsessiveness, 196
O'Neal, Shaquille, 161, 162
Ordering cycle, knowing, 191–92

Past and future
   researching, 105–15
   words about, 107–8, 139–40
Point, getting to, 152, 163
Power referrals, 198
Presentation
   body language for, 166
   building rapport during, 164–68
   charts and, 196–97
   demonstrations and, 196
   dressing for, 166, 168
   ending, 190
   follow-up for, 189–94
   importance of, 8–9
   interview and, 196

listening skills for, 145–50, 160–61
note taking and, 197
overcoming objections, 171–82
parts of, 152–56, 163–68
preparing, 160–61, 164
prospecting and, 151–68
reasons for, 157–68
starting off right, 154–56
storytelling for, 160–64
strategies for, 143
summarizing, 152
tips for, 151–68, 196–98
using what works, 153–54
warm-ups for, 155–56
words for, 154, 156, 159
Price, introducing, 159, 197
Price objections, 173, 177–79, 195
Promises, keeping, 199
Prospecting
   cold calls for, 11–21
   for decision-makers, 106, 110–15,
      118, 138–39
   importance of, 8–9, 195–96
   interactions and, 146
   listening and, 145–50
   monitoring results for, 195
   note taking for, 148–49
   presentation skills and, 151–68
   research and, 105–15
   small talk and, 139–41
   successful prospecting, 12, 146
   visiting prospects, 196
   words for, 9–12
Purchase cycle, knowing, 191–92

Questions
essential questions, 82–92, 112–13
framing, 82–104
general questions, 98–99
for interview, 81–92
leading questions, 99–101
qualifying statements for, 17–18
responses to, 102–4
six-question model, 82–92, 112–13
for small talk, 118–22, 125–30,
132–34
specific questions, 99

Rapport, building, 74, 119, 164–68,
197–98
Research tips, 105–15
Responses
common responses, 58–66
feedback from, 164, 172–73
in kind, 13–14
learning from, 122–26
listening to, 66–68
"no" responses, 58–66, 181–82,
185–87
ritual responses, 102–4
to sales calls, 57–70
sample responses, 69–70
words for, 61–66
Results, monitoring, 195
"Right person," 106, 118, 138–39. *See
also* Decision-makers
Rules for success, 195–99

Sale, parts of, 8
Sales cycle, knowing, 191–94
Salespeople, as helpers, 146–48

Salespeople, successful, 146
Sales, successful, 12, 146, 195–99
Sample cold call, 20–21
Sample e-mails, 48–50, 55–56
Sample framing questions, 104
Sample interviews, 90–92
Sample listening scenarios, 149–50
Sample objections, 69–70, 176, 178–
79, 182
Sample sales dialogues
for first appointment, 202–8
for second appointment, 209–15
for third appointment, 216–17
Sample small talk, 120–31, 134–37,
139–41
Sample voicemail messages, 38–39
Scripts, value of, 19–20, 118
Simon, Paul, 155
Six-question model, 82–92, 112–13
Small talk
art of, 117–42
learning from, 122–32, 138–39
on past history, 139–41
prospecting and, 139–41
questions for, 118–22, 125–30,
132–34
samples of, 120–31, 134–37,
139–41
words for, 120, 127
Storytelling, 160–64
Success, rules for, 195–99
Successful cold calls, 20–21
Successful sales, 12, 146, 195–99
Successful salespeople, 146

"Tactical" selling, 89
Team calling, 31–33
Telephone tag, 33–35, 37–38
"Thinking about it" objections, 174–76
Truth, telling, 61–66
"Turnaround-oriented" selling, 89

Unsuccessful salespeople, 146. *See also* Successful sales

Visual aids, 196
Voicemail
    for cold calls, 35–38
    effective messages for, 23–39
    examples of, 25–26, 28–31
    follow-up for, 28, 38–39
    sample voicemail, 38–39
    for team calling, 31–33
    telephone tag and, 33–35, 37–38
    words for, 26

Words and phrases. *See also* Sample dialogues
    for asking for sale, 184–85
    for beginning presentation, 154
    for calling purposes, 16
    for closing deal, 184–85
    for e-mail messages, 47, 50–51, 54
    for finding what went wrong, 182
    for follow-ups, 28, 191
    for framing questions, 97
    for getting appointment, 19
    for identifying self, 14–15
    for "I'm happy" response, 61
    for interview, 71–74, 79, 133–34

for introducing self, 13–14
for leaving message, 26
for listening, 147–48
for "not interested" response, 62
for overcoming objections, 175, 178, 182
for past and future, 107–8, 139–40
for phone calls, 26, 28, 35
for presentations, 154, 156, 159
for prospecting, 9–12
for questioning statement, 17
for research questions, 107–8, 139–40
for "send literature" response, 66
for small talk, 120, 127
for team calling, 31–32
for telephone tag, 35
for "too busy" response, 64
for using names, 30
for voicemail messages, 26